the
CHOCOLATE
LOVER'S
Cookbook

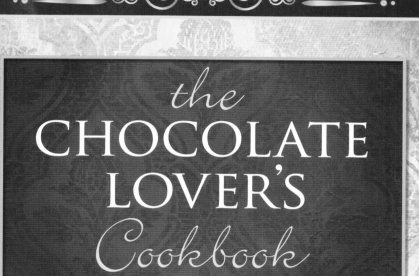

the
CHOCOLATE
LOVER'S
Cookbook

More than 100 sumptuous recipes

Reader's
Digest

CONTENTS

THE JOY OF CHOCOLATE

Chocolate — is there a more enticing food?
Both indulgent luxury and everyday treat,
it's something many of us can't live without.

*The Latin name of the cacao tree translates
as 'food of the gods' — and who would argue?*

DELECTABLE CHOCOLATE

Chocolate has been cultivated for at least 3000 years, and is now one of the world's most popular foods. Whether you're after a special-occasion dessert or a lunchbox cookie, you're sure to find something tempting in this book. There are classic recipes and family favourites such as Mud Cake, Choc-chip Biscuits and Chocolate Mousse, plus new and contemporary recipes such as Triple-Chocolate Brownie Cookies and Chocolate Cherry Cupcakes. We've also included plenty of hints and tips to ensure success.

WHAT MAKES A GOOD CHOCOLATE?

The key things to look for in chocolate are cocoa solids and cocoa butter. The more cocoa solids it contains, the deeper and more intense the chocolate flavour will be. Check the wrapping: any chocolate containing less than 50 per cent cocoa solids has little real chocolate taste; one with 70 per cent or more will have a much stronger, finer chocolate flavour.

The more cocoa butter the chocolate contains, the softer it is, melting more easily and having a smooth, luscious 'mouth feel'. Sometimes cheaper vegetable oils are substituted for cocoa butter, reducing the flavour and coarsening the texture. Check the ingredients list, since

these are shown in order of volume. If vegetable oil comes higher on the list than cocoa butter, the chocolate is of inferior quality.

As a general rule, the thinner and smaller the pieces of chocolate, the finer it will be. Another way of identifying good chocolate is by how smooth it feels on the tongue. Very fine chocolate with a superior flavour is expensive, but you do not have to use as much to get an intense chocolate taste, so it is a good idea to buy the best you can find or afford.

Buy from a shop with good turnover and look for clean, neat packaging — a sign the chocolate is fresh.

TYPES OF CHOCOLATE

There are various types of chocolate products. The more cocoa solids each contains, the more bitter and chocolatey it is. The different types are not always interchangeable in cooking, as they have different ratios of cocoa butter and cocoa solids, which can affect the texture, moisture and flavour of the recipe.

The following are general guidelines only, as the ratios of ingredients in various types of chocolate vary from country to country.

UNSWEETENED CHOCOLATE

Also known as baking chocolate or bitter chocolate, unsweetened chocolate contains cocoa solids without added sugar or flavouring. Bitter, grainy and difficult to melt, it is used mainly by bakers and manufacturers of chocolate products rather than by home cooks. Professionals prefer it as they can completely control the sugar content of the finished dish. For the home cook, in recipes that specify unsweetened chocolate, replace each 30 g (1 oz) unsweetened chocolate with 2 tablespoons unsweetened cocoa powder plus 3 teaspoons unsalted butter.

DARK CHOCOLATE

Also known as plain chocolate, dark chocolate contains varying percentages of cocoa, plus sugar and fat. It is suitable for both eating and baking. Recipes specifying dark chocolate will be most successful if made with a chocolate that has at least 50 per cent cocoa solids.

BITTERSWEET AND SEMISWEET CHOCOLATE

Both types of dark chocolate, these have a high proportion of cocoa solids and little sugar (though semisweet has slightly more than bittersweet). They can be eaten as is, if you like bitter chocolate, or used interchangeably in cooking.

COUVERTURE

Couverture is a type of chocolate used by professional confectioners and patissiers, but it is also suited to the home cook. It contains more cocoa butter than ordinary chocolate and so melts and spreads easily.

It also contains cocoa solids, sugar and, in the case of milk couverture, milk powder. Couverture has a high shine, a rich flavour and a brittle texture. It is used to make chocolates and to coat chocolate cakes and desserts. For use in coating, it first has to be tempered (see page 10). For recipes that require melted couverture to be combined with other ingredients, it does not need to be tempered first. Dark, milk and white couverture are available.

COOKING CHOCOLATE

The quality of cooking chocolate can vary widely. Choose a brand with a high percentage of cocoa solids and little or no vegetable oil (this should be absent from, or low down on, the list of ingredients on the package). Types containing a large ratio of vegetable oil will have an inferior flavour or texture and are sometimes known as compound chocolate. Poor-quality chocolate such as compound chocolate lacks the lushness and intense flavour of true chocolate, and in most cases is best avoided.

MILK CHOCOLATE

Milk chocolate combines 20–30 per cent cocoa solids and milk (either fresh, powdered or condensed). It is the most common eating chocolate, but is less widely used in cooking and should not be substituted for dark chocolate in baking, as it will not give the same result.

WHITE CHOCOLATE

This is not technically chocolate at all, as it contains no cocoa solids. It is made from cocoa butter (and/or, in cheaper types, vegetable fat), sugar, milk powder and vanilla. It is creamy-white in colour and very sweet, without the bitterness or the true chocolate taste of other types of chocolate. It is particularly sensitive to heat and can be difficult to handle.

COCOA POWDER

If cocoa solids are pulverised and sieved, unsweetened (or natural) cocoa powder is the result. Cocoa powder can be used in baking or mixed with hot water or milk to make a drink. When used in baking, cocoa is usually sifted with the other dry ingredients, or it can be blended into a paste with cold water.

Cocoa powder with added sugar is usually sold as drinking chocolate. It should not be substituted for unsweetened cocoa in recipes, as the additional sugar and flavourings will affect the result.

DUTCH COCOA

Dutch (or Dutch-process) cocoa powder is unsweetened cocoa powder that has been processed with an alkali (bicarbonate of soda/baking soda) to neutralise its natural acidity. It dissolves more easily than natural cocoa powder, and is rich and dark. It is considered the best type of cocoa powder to use in cooking.

TIPS AND TECHNIQUES

Storing

Store chocolate and cocoa powder in a cool, dry, airy place away from strong odours. Unless you live in a tropical climate, chocolate should not be refrigerated, as the atmosphere is too cold and moist for it. If you need to refrigerate chocolate, allow it to come to room temperature before breaking or melting it.

Dark chocolate will keep for about a year; milk chocolate, about 6 months. Chocolate keeps better in a large block or thick chunks than in small pieces. For this reason, buy chocolate chips, bits or melts as needed.

Chocolate can be frozen for longer storage. Wrap it well in foil and thaw it in the same wrapping so it can reabsorb the moisture it lost while freezing.

Incorrectly stored chocolate may develop a white coating known as 'bloom'. This looks unsightly, but the flavour is unaffected and the chocolate is still edible, and can be melted and used in baking.

Tempering

Tempering is a technique in which chocolate is stabilised by melting then cooling it to a particular temperature. For most recipes, it is not necessary to temper chocolate. Tempering is mainly done when making confectionery or using chocolate as coatings or decorations. Most bought chocolate is already 'in temper'.

MELTING AND DIPPING

Care must be taken when melting chocolate, but it is worth the effort. Melted chocolate can be used in a variety of chocolate desserts, cakes, ice-cream and confectionery.

MELTING ON THE STOVE

1 *Chop the chocolate finely with a sharp, dry knife on a dry cutting board. Fill a saucepan one-third full of water and bring it to a boil, then reduce heat to a simmer. Put the chocolate into a heatproof bowl and set it over the saucepan to melt slowly.*

2 *The base of the bowl must not touch the water. The water should be barely simmering; ensure no steam comes into contact with the chocolate, otherwise it will stiffen and be unusable. Leave bowl to stand; stir mixture occasionally until it is very smooth.*

MELTING IN THE MICROWAVE

1 *Break the chocolate into small pieces in a microwave-safe bowl. Place on the edge of the turntable. Melt on the Defrost setting for approximately 1-minute cycles, stopping and stirring with a plastic spoon after each cycle, until melted.*

2 *Check amounts over 250 g (8 oz) after 2 minutes, initially; check smaller amounts after 30 seconds.*

DIPPING NUTS AND FRUIT

1 *Choose large, perfect nuts (here, Brazil nuts) and dip them one at a time. Place the nut on a small fork then lower it into the cooled, melted chocolate. Lift it straight out again and gently tap the fork on the side of the bowl to remove excess chocolate.*

2 *Using a toothpick, push the nut gently off onto a tray lined with baking (parchment) paper.*

3 *Small pieces of fruit can be dipped in the same way, after being peeled, cut, then patted dry with paper towels.*

4 *For half-dipped fruits choose those with stems or stalks such as cape gooseberries, strawberries and cherries, or dried or glacé fruits such as apricots, prunes or stem ginger. Holding the stem or the top of the fruit, lower it halfway into the melted chocolate.*

5 *Lift it straight out, shake off the excess chocolate then place it on trays lined with baking (parchment) paper to set. When the fruits are set, store in a cool, dry place until ready to serve.*

GLAZING A CAKE

A glaze is a thin, glossy coating of chocolate with either cream (as here) or icing (confectioners') sugar, hot water and sometimes butter, that is poured over the cake. This amount of glaze is enough to coat the top and sides of a 20–23 cm (8–9 inch) cake.

1 *Grate or finely chop 250 g (8 oz) dark chocolate and put it in a heatproof bowl. Heat ½ cup (125 ml) pouring cream just to boiling point. Pour over the chocolate in the bowl and stir gently (so you don't incorporate air bubbles) until the chocolate has melted and the mixture is smooth. Set aside until cooled to a coating consistency, stirring occasionally.*

2 *Set the cake on a wire rack and place the rack over a baking tray. Pour the glaze slowly and evenly all over the cake, allowing it to flow down the sides. Any drips can be poured back into the bowl and reused if need be.*

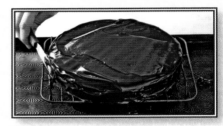

3 *Smooth the top first with a palette knife or metal spatula, then smooth the sides.*

DECORATING

Elegant adornments made from fine chocolate add the perfect finishing touch to homemade cakes.

CHOCOLATE BARK

1 *Spread melted chocolate on a baking tray lined with baking (parchment) paper. Chill for 30 minutes. Break into rectangles.*

2 *Press chocolate pieces into the icing (frosting) on the cake, arranging them so that they resemble bark.*

ORNAMENTS

To make ornaments, pipe melted chocolate onto baking (parchment) paper. Allow to dry, then ease the chocolate off the paper.

Melted chocolate can be used in a simple glaze to spread over a cake, or made into a variety of attractive decorations.

SCROLLS

1 *Pour melted chocolate onto a marble slab, chilled baking tray or another smooth, cool surface.*

2 *Spread it with a palette knife to not more than 3 mm (¹/₈ inch) thick and leave in a cool place until set but not completely hard.*

3 *Holding a long, firm knife or scraper at an angle of 45° to the chocolate, push away from you to scrape off long curls. Hold the tip of the knife securely and scrape in a quarter-circle movement.*

CURLS

1 *Be sure chocolate is at room temperature. Draw the blade of a vegetable peeler across the entire bar, pressing down firmly.*

2 *Lift the curls with a toothpick or skewer. (Using your fingers might melt the curls.)*

LEAVES

1 *Wash some firm, unsprayed, non-poisonous leaves (such as bay leaves) and rub dry. Brush one side of the leaf with melted chocolate or couverture.*

2 *Allow the leaves to dry with the uncoated side down. Pull the leaf off the chocolate coating, working from the stem towards the tip.*

CAKES AND TARTS

CHOCOLATE MUD CAKE

2 cups (270 g) lightly packed soft
  brown sugar
1½ cups (375 ml) strong black
  coffee
250 g (8 oz) butter
200 g (7 oz) dark chocolate,
  chopped
2 eggs
250 g (8 oz) plain (all-purpose)
  flour
30 g (1 oz) self-raising flour
¼ cup (30 g) unsweetened cocoa
  powder
1 cup (150 g) blueberries and
  raspberries, to serve (optional)
whipped cream, to serve
  (optional)

CHOCOLATE GLAZE

½ cup (125 ml) pouring cream
250 g (8 oz) dark chocolate,
  chopped

•→ **PREPARATION** 20 minutes plus
    cooling
•→ **COOKING** About 1 hour
•→ **SERVES** 12

1 Preheat the oven to 150°C (300°F/Gas 2).
Lightly grease a 23 cm (9 inch) cake tin and line
the base and side with baking (parchment) paper.

2 Combine sugar, coffee, butter and chocolate
in a saucepan and heat gently, stirring until the
sugar has dissolved and the ingredients are well
combined. Do not allow to boil. Transfer the
mixture to a bowl and cool for 30 minutes.

3 Meanwhile, sift together the flours and cocoa
into another bowl. Add the eggs to the cooled
chocolate mixture and beat well, then stir in the
flour mixture until well combined.

4 Pour into the prepared cake tin and bake for
about 1 hour, or until a skewer inserted in the
centre comes out almost clean. (As this is a very
moist cake it will not set completely in the centre,
but will firm up as it cools.) Cool in the pan.

5 Meanwhile, make the glaze. Heat the cream
in a small saucepan over low heat. Put the
chocolate in a heatproof bowl and pour the hot
cream over. Stir gently until chocolate is melted
and mixture is glossy and smooth. Let stand for
20–30 minutes, or until spreadable. Spread the
glaze smoothly over the top and side of the cake,
then let stand for 10 minutes to set. Top with
fresh fruit and serve with cream, if desired.

FLOURLESS CHOCOLATE CAKE

250 g (8 oz) dark chocolate,
    broken into pieces
125 g (4 oz) unsalted butter, diced
6 large eggs, separated
½ cup (115 g) caster (superfine)
    sugar
2½ cups (250 g) almond meal
    (ground almonds)

ICING

250 g (8 oz) dark chocolate
1 cup (250 ml) pouring cream

···• PREPARATION 40 minutes
···• COOKING 45 minutes
···• SERVES 12

🐚 Alternatively in Step 2,
melt the butter and chocolate
in a microwave on low power
in short bursts. Stir after each
burst, until smooth.

1 Preheat the oven to 180°C (350°F/Gas 4). Line the base and side of a 23 cm (9 inch) springform cake tin with baking (parchment) paper.

2 Melt the chocolate and butter in a heatproof bowl over a saucepan of barely simmering water, stirring occasionally. Remove from the heat; cool slightly.

3 In a medium bowl using an electric mixer, beat the egg yolks and sugar until pale and creamy. Add the melted chocolate mixture and almonds and stir well.

4 In a separate bowl, beat the eggwhites on high speed until stiff peaks form. Fold into the chocolate mixture, pour into the tin and spread level. Bake for 45 minutes, or until firm and a skewer inserted in the centre comes out clean.

5 Cool completely in the tin on a wire rack.

6 To make the icing, break the chocolate into a food processor; process until finely chopped. Transfer to a heatproof bowl.

7 Heat the cream in a saucepan until scalded (almost boiling) and pour over the chocolate. Stir until the mixture is smooth.

8 Place the cold cake on a wire rack set over a large plate or baking tray to catch the drips. Pour the icing over it and leave to set.

FLOURLESS CHOCOLATE ALMOND CAKE

This moist cake presents an alternative to the traditional flour-based cake. Its mild chocolate taste is jazzed up with whipped cream and berries.

3 eggs, separated
¾ cup (115 g) whole unblanched almonds
2 tablespoons sugar, plus ⅓ cup (75 g) extra
¼ cup (60 ml) hot water
¼ cup (30 g) unsweetened cocoa powder
1½ teaspoons vanilla extract
pinch cream of tartar
pinch salt
chocolate syrup (optional)

⤳ PREPARATION 35 minutes
⤳ COOKING 30 minutes
⤳ SERVES 4

1 Grease a 15 cm (6 inch) springform cake tin. Preheat the oven to 180°C (350°F/Gas 4).

2 Let the eggs stand at room temperature for 30 minutes. Meanwhile, in a food processor, combine the almonds and 2 tablespoons sugar; process in short bursts until ground. Combine the water and cocoa; set aside.

3 In a small bowl using an electric mixer, beat egg yolks until slightly thickened. Gradually add remaining sugar, beating until thick and pale. Blend in the almond mixture, cocoa mixture and vanilla. In another bowl, beat the eggwhites, cream of tartar and salt on high speed until stiff peaks form. Fold the eggwhites into the batter.

4 Pour into tin, place tin on a tray and bake for 35 minutes, or until the cake springs back when lightly touched. Cool in the tin on a wire rack for 10 minutes. Carefully run a knife around edge of tin to loosen; leave cake in tin until completely cold. Drizzle with chocolate syrup if desired.

FUDGY FLOURLESS CHOCOLATE CAKE WITH GANACHE

4 eggs, separated
150 g (5 oz) butter, cubed
½ cup (110 g) sugar
250 g (8 oz) dark chocolate,
    chopped
2 teaspoons vanilla extract
¼ cup (30 g) finely ground
    pecans, toasted
Chocolate Ganache (see below)
sliced strawberries and fresh mint,
    to garnish (optional)

PREPARATION 20 minutes
COOKING 50 minutes
SERVES 16

1 Preheat the oven to 180°C (350°F/Gas 4). Grease a 23 cm (9 inch) springform cake tin.

2 Let the eggs stand at room temperature for 30 minutes. Meanwhile, in a heavy saucepan, melt the butter, ¼ cup (55 g) sugar and the chocolate over low heat, stirring constantly. Cool to lukewarm.

3 In a large bowl using an electric mixer, beat egg yolks on high speed for about 3 minutes, or until thick and pale. Beat in the vanilla. Gradually beat in the pecans and chocolate mixture.

4 In a small bowl and with clean beaters, beat the eggwhites on medium speed until soft peaks form. Gradually add remaining sugar, 1 tablespoon at a time, beating on high speed until stiff peaks form. Stir a small amount of eggwhites into chocolate mixture. Fold in remaining whites.

5 Pour into the prepared tin, place tin on a baking tray and bake for 40–50 minutes, or until a skewer inserted in the centre comes out with a few moist crumbs. Cool in the tin on a wire rack for 20 minutes.

6 Carefully run a knife around the edge of the tin to loosen; remove the side of the pan and cool cake completely. Spread the cake with the chocolate ganache. Garnish with strawberries and mint, if desired.

CHOCOLATE GANACHE

1 cup (6 oz) dark (semisweet)
    chocolate chips
⅔ cup (160 ml) thickened (heavy/double)
    whipping cream

Place chocolate chips in a small bowl. In a small saucepan, bring the cream just to the boil. Pour over the chocolate; stir until smooth. Chill, stirring occasionally, until mixture reaches a spreadable consistency.

CHOCOLATE SUPREME CAKE

1½ cups (330 g) raw (demerara)
  sugar
250 g (8 oz) unbleached plain
  (all-purpose) flour
¾ cup (90 g) unsweetened cocoa
  powder
1½ teaspoons bicarbonate of soda
  (baking soda)
1½ teaspoons baking powder
4 eggwhites
1 cup (250 ml) low-fat milk
½ cup (135 g) apple sauce
½ teaspoon vanilla extract
1 cup (250 ml) boiling water
fresh berries, to serve (optional)

ICING

3 tablespoons low-fat cream
  cheese
1 tablespoon low-fat sour cream
½ cup (60 g) unsweetened cocoa
  powder
1½ cups (350 g) caster (superfine)
  sugar
1 teaspoon vanilla extract

•➤ PREPARATION 30 minutes
•➤ COOKING 35 minutes
•➤ SERVES 14

1 Preheat the oven to 180°C (350°F/Gas 4).
Grease a deep 23 cm (9 inch) cake tin and
dust with flour, shaking out the excess.

2 In a bowl, combine the sugar, flour, cocoa,
bicarbonate of soda and baking powder. Add
the eggwhites, milk, apple sauce, vanilla and
water, and beat with an electric mixer on
medium speed for 2 minutes. Pour into the
prepared tin and bake for 35 minutes, or until a
skewer inserted in the centre comes out clean.
Turn out onto a wire rack to cool completely.

3 Meanwhile, in a bowl beat the cream cheese,
sour cream, cocoa, sugar and vanilla until
smooth. Using a spatula, ice the cake. Top with
the fruit, if using. Serve at room temperature.

Chocolate cake is a special treat. But this
one, despite being rich, gooey and abundantly
delicious, is made with ingredients, such as apple
sauce and eggwhites, that keep the 'sin' quotient
low. A handful of fresh berries or sliced seasonal
fruit elevates this cake from super to spectacular.

HEART-SHAPED CHOCOLATE CAKE

185 g (6½ oz) plain (all-purpose)
   flour
1 teaspoon baking powder, sifted
⅔ cup (145 g) caster (superfine)
   sugar
¼ cup (30 g) unsweetened cocoa
   powder, plus extra for dusting
125 g (4 oz) butter, melted
2 eggs
¾ cup (180 ml) milk
1 teaspoon vanilla essence

CHOCOLATE BUTTERCREAM

125 g (4 oz) unsalted butter,
   softened
1 cup (125 g) icing
   (confectioners') sugar, sifted
125 g (4 oz) dark chocolate,
   melted, cooled slightly

•- PREPARATION 15 minutes
•- COOKING 1 hour
•- SERVES 6

1 Preheat the oven to 180°C (350°F/Gas 4) or
160°C (320°F/Gas 2–3) fan-forced. Grease and
flour a 4 cup (1 litre) capacity silicone heart-
shaped mould.

2 Sift flour, baking powder, sugar and cocoa into
a medium bowl and mix until well combined.
Add the butter, eggs, milk and vanilla and whisk
until smooth. Pour into the prepared mould and
cook for 1 hour, or until cooked when a skewer
inserted in the centre comes out clean. Cool
completely in the mould before turning out.

3 To make the buttercream icing, beat the butter
until light and creamy. Gradually beat in the icing
sugar and continue beating until the mixture is
light and fluffy. Add the melted chocolate and
beat until combined.

4 Spread the buttercream over the cake. Allow to
set then dust with cocoa and serve.

*This simple-to-make mixture is baked in a
heart-shaped mould for romantic appeal —
perfect for a birthday or Valentine's Day.*

QUICK CHOCOLATE CAKE

*W*hen all you need is an old-fashioned, simple chocolate cake, rather than a fancy affair, try this microwave recipe. It's quick and easy.

¾ cup (185 g) butter, softened
¾ cup (170 g) caster (superfine) sugar
¼ teaspoon vanilla extract
3 tablespoons milk
3 medium eggs
185 g (6½ oz) self-raising flour
1 teaspoon baking powder
4 tablespoons (50 g) unsweetened cocoa powder

CHOCOLATE ICING

2 tablespoons butter
2 tablespoons water
1 cup (140 g) icing (confectioners') sugar
2 tablespoons unsweetened cocoa powder

⊷ PREPARATION 10 minutes
⊷ COOKING 10 minutes
⊷ SERVES 8

1 Line the base of a 20 cm (8 inch) microwave-safe cake tin with baking (parchment) paper.

2 In a medium bowl using an electric mixer, beat the butter, sugar, vanilla, milk and eggs on low speed until smooth; do not overbeat. Sift in the flour, baking powder and cocoa and mix well.

3 Pour the mixture into the prepared tin. Cook in the microwave oven on medium–high power (70 per cent) for 10 minutes, or until just cooked. Cool in the tin on a wire rack for 5 minutes, then turn out onto the rack to cool completely.

4 To prepare the icing, melt the butter and water in a microwave-safe bowl. Whisk in the icing sugar and cocoa. Allow to cool until thickened to a spreadable consistency, then spread over the cooled cake.

WHITE CHOCOLATE CAKE

175 g (6 oz) white chocolate, chopped

4 eggwhites

1 teaspoon vanilla extract

1 cup (250 ml) milk

300 g (10 oz) self-raising flour

250 g (8 oz) caster (superfine) sugar

1 tablespoon baking powder

125 g (4 oz) unsalted butter, softened

pinch salt

CREAM CHEESE ICING

60 g (2 oz) cream cheese, softened

30 g (1 oz) unsalted butter, softened

1/2 teaspoon vanilla extract

3/4 cup (90 g) icing (confectioners') sugar

1 cup (60 g) flaked coconut

• PREPARATION 20 minutes

• COOKING 50 minutes

• SERVES 12

1 Preheat the oven to 180°C (350°F/Gas 4). Grease a 25 cm (10 inch) springform cake tin and line the base with baking (parchment) paper.

2 Melt the chocolate in a heatproof bowl set over a saucepan of simmering water. Remove from the heat and stir until smooth. Allow to cool.

3 In a separate bowl, lightly whisk the eggwhites, vanilla and 1/2 cup (125 ml) milk.

4 In a large bowl using an electric mixer, beat the flour, sugar, baking powder, butter, salt and remaining milk until light and fluffy. Fold in the eggwhite mixture, then the cooled white chocolate until combined. Spoon the mixture into the tin and bake for 45–50 minutes, or until a skewer inserted in the centre comes out clean.

5 Cool in the tin on a wire rack for about 10 minutes, then turn out onto the rack to cool completely.

6 Combine the icing ingredients in a bowl and beat well. Ice the top and side of the cooled cake. Sprinkle the flaked coconut on top.

QUICK CHOCOLATE CAKE
WITH RASPBERRIES

185 g (6 oz) plain (all-purpose)
   flour
1/2 cup (60 g) unsweetened cocoa
   powder, plus extra for dusting
1 teaspoon baking powder
1/2 teaspoon bicarbonate of soda
   (baking soda)
salt, to taste (optional)
250 g (8 oz) sugar
1/2 cup (135 g) apple sauce
1 egg or 2 eggwhites
1 cup (250 ml) low-fat milk or
   water
2 teaspoons vanilla extract
1/4 cup (80 g) seedless raspberry
   jam
fresh raspberries, to serve
icing (confectioners') sugar,
   for dusting

➤ PREPARATION 15 minutes
➤ COOKING 45 minutes
➤ SERVES 9

1 Preheat the oven to 180°C (350°F/Gas 4).
Lightly grease a 20 cm (8 inch) square cake tin.
Dust with cocoa powder, shaking out the excess.

2 In a medium bowl, sift together the flour,
cocoa, baking powder, bicarbonate of soda and
salt. Stir to combine.

3 In a large bowl using an electric mixer, beat
the sugar, apple sauce and egg or eggwhites on
low speed until very smooth. Beat in the milk
and vanilla until just blended. Add the flour
mixture and beat until just blended.

4 Spoon the mixture into the prepared tin
and bake for 40–45 minutes, or until a skewer
inserted in the centre comes out clean. Cool in
the tin on a wire rack for 10 minutes, then turn
the cake out onto the rack to cool completely.

5 To serve, melt the jam in a saucepan over
low heat. Brush over the top of the cooled cake.
Top with raspberries and dust with icing sugar.

Who says dessert has to be sinful to taste terrific? This lip-smackingly delicious treat has only 2 grams of fat per serving.

DEVIL'S FOOD CAKE

*W*arning: this cake is wickedly indulgent!
To make it slightly less sinful, you can replace
the chocolate ganache with a simple chocolate icing.

350 g (12 oz) self-raising flour

¾ cup (90 g) unsweetened cocoa
powder

1 teaspoon bicarbonate of soda
(baking soda)

1½ cups (345 g) caster (superfine)
sugar

160 g (5½ oz) butter

2 teaspoons vanilla extract

3 eggs, beaten

CHOCOLATE GANACHE

¾ cup (180 ml) thickened (heavy/
double) whipping cream

200 g (7 oz) dark chocolate,
roughly chopped

⁕ PREPARATION 20 minutes

⁕ COOKING 1 hour

⁕ SERVES 12

1 Preheat the oven to 180°C (350°F/Gas 4). Grease a 23 cm (9 inch) cake tin and line the base and side with baking (parchment) paper.

2 Sift the flour, cocoa and bicarbonate of soda into a large bowl. Stir in the sugar until well combined.

3 Combine the butter, vanilla and 1 cup (250 ml) water in a saucepan over medium heat. Stir until the butter has melted, then add to the flour mixture and whisk until well combined. Add the eggs and whisk until blended.

4 Spoon the mixture into the prepared tin and smooth the top. Bake for 45–60 minutes, or until a skewer inserted in the centre of the cake comes out clean. Remove the cake from the oven and cool in the tin on a wire rack for 5 minutes, then turn out onto the rack to cool completely.

5 To make the icing, heat the cream in a small saucepan over low–medium heat. When bubbles are beginning to form around the edge of the saucepan, remove the pan from the heat and stir in the chocolate until melted and smooth. Transfer to a bowl and stand at room temperature, stirring occasionally, until the icing is of a spreadable consistency.

6 When the cake is cold, spread the icing over the top.

Chocolate ganache is simply a mixture of chocolate and cream, melted together then allowed to cool and thicken. The ratio of cream to chocolate determines how thick the ganache will be. More cream, and the ganache will be of a pouring or spreading consistency; less cream, and the ganache will set hard enough that decorative shapes can be cut from it. See pages 21 and 32 for other ganache recipes.

DEATH BY CHOCOLATE

·–·· **PREPARATION** 1–2 hours plus chilling

·–·· **COOKING** About 2 hours

·–·· **SERVES** 12

CHOCOLATE MERINGUE

2 large eggwhites

¼ cup (55 g) caster (superfine) sugar

⅓ cup (40 g) icing (confectioners')
    sugar

1½ tablespoons (15 g) unsweetened
    cocoa powder

SPONGE CAKE

6 large eggs

185 g (6 oz) sugar

125 g (4 oz) self-raising flour

¼ cup (30 g) cocoa powder

2 tablespoons cornflour (cornstarch)

75 g (2½ oz) unsalted butter, melted

GANACHE TOPPING

¼ cup (60 g) sugar

60 g (2 oz) unsalted butter

2 cups (500 ml) cream

2 tablespoons dark rum

500 g (1 lb) dark chocolate, melted

MOUSSE FILLING

125 g (4 oz) unsalted butter

250 g (8 oz) dark chocolate

3 tablespoons dark rum

2 large eggs, separated

300 ml (10 fl oz) thickened (heavy/
    double) whipping cream

chocolate leaves (see page 13)
    and icing (confectioners') sugar,
    to decorate

1 To make the meringue, preheat the oven to 120°C (250°F/Gas ¼–½). Line the base and side of a 23 cm (9 inch) springform cake tin with baking (parchment) paper.

2 In a bowl using an electric mixer, beat the eggwhites on high speed until stiff, then gradually whisk in the caster sugar. Sift the icing sugar and the cocoa over the mixture and gently fold in. Spread the mixture into the prepared tin and bake for 1–1½ hours, or until the meringue is crisp and dry.

3 To make the sponge cake, increase the oven temperature to 180°C (350°F/Gas 4). Grease a 23 cm (9 inch) springform cake tin and line the base and side with baking paper.

4 In a bowl using an electric mixer, beat the eggs and sugar until creamy and thick enough to leave a ribbon-like trail when the beaters are lifted from the mixture.

5 Sift the flour, cocoa and cornflour together then gently fold into the egg mixture a little at a time, alternating with the melted butter. Spread the mixture into the prepared tin and bake for about 30 minutes, or until the cake is quite firm to the touch in the centre.

6 Remove the cake from the oven, allow to cool in the tin on a wire rack for

10 minutes, then turn out onto the rack to cool completely. Carefully slice the cold cake in half horizontally.

7 To make the ganache, heat the sugar, butter, cream and rum until the sugar has dissolved. Stir in the melted chocolate, then chill for 30 minutes, or until set.

8 To make the mousse filling, melt the butter, chocolate and rum in a heatproof bowl over a saucepan of simmering water, stirring occasionally. Cool slightly. Beat in egg yolks, then fold in the cream.

9 Beat the eggwhites using an electric mixer until they form stiff peaks, then fold them into the chocolate mixture. Leave to set for 30 minutes to 1 hour.

10 When the mousse has set, assemble the cake. Put one sponge cake layer on a plate, spread half the mousse on it, then put the meringue layer on top. Spread the remaining mousse on top of the meringue. Top with the other cake layer.

11 Spread the ganache over the cake, decorate with chocolate leaves and dust with icing sugar. Serve immediately or chill for a few hours.

MARBLE CAKE

250 g (8 oz) butter

1¼ cups (275 g) caster (superfine)
   sugar

few drops vanilla extract

4 eggs

¾ cup (180 ml) milk, plus
   1 tablespoon extra

335 g (11 oz) self-raising flour,
   sifted

1 tablespoon unsweetened cocoa
   powder, sifted

⌁ PREPARATION 20 minutes

⌁ COOKING 70 minutes

⌁ SERVES 8–12

1 Preheat the oven to 180°C (350°F/Gas 4).
Line a 17 x 10 x 9 cm deep (6½ x 4 x 3½ inch
deep) loaf tin (bar pan) with a capacity of 6 cups
(1.5 litres).

2 Beat the butter in a large bowl using an electric
mixer until creamy. Add the sugar (reserving
1 tablespoon) and vanilla and beat until well
combined and pale and fluffy. Add the eggs, one
at a time, beating well after each addition. Add
the milk in batches to the batter, alternating it
with the flour, mixing well after each addition.

3 Spoon one-third of the batter into a bowl and
stir in the cocoa, reserved sugar and extra milk.

4 Drop spoonfuls of both batters into the
prepared tin and use a skewer to swirl through
the batter to create a marbled effect. Tap the tin
on the bench to smooth the top and bake for
70 minutes, or until a skewer comes out clean.
Cool in the tin on a wire rack for 10 minutes,
then turn the cake out onto the rack to cool
completely.

⁓ For an extra treat, spread melted chocolate
over the cooled cake and scatter the top with
chocolate sprinkles.

Cocoa powder gives this cake a rich chocolate flavour, but for an extra chocolate boost, try adding a little chopped chocolate to the batter.

MARBLE RING CAKE

300 g (10 oz) self-raising flour
1 teaspoon baking powder
250 g (8 oz) butter, softened
200 g (7 oz) sugar
1 teaspoon vanilla extract
pinch salt
4 eggs
4 tablespoons milk
$\frac{1}{3}$ cup (50 g) chopped almonds
100 g (3½ oz) dark chocolate,
    finely grated
2 tablespoons rum

GLAZE

200 g (7 oz) ready-made dark
    chocolate icing or glaze
100 g (3½ oz) ready-made white
    chocolate icing or glaze

·•· PREPARATION 40 minutes
·•· COOKING 45 minutes
·•· SERVES 12–14

Here is a particularly luxurious version of the classic marble cake — chocolate and almonds have been added and it is glazed with dark chocolate and white icing.

1 Preheat the oven to 180°C (350°F/ Gas 4). Thoroughly grease a 23 cm (9 inch) fluted ring or bundt tin. Sift the flour and baking powder into a bowl.

2 In another bowl, using an electric mixer, beat the butter until fluffy, then beat in the sugar, vanilla and salt until pale and creamy. Mix in the eggs, one at a time, beating well after each addition.

3 Stir the flour mixture, 1 tablespoonful at a time, into the butter and egg mixture. Add the milk and mix until just blended. Place half of the batter in a separate bowl. Stir the almonds into one half of the batter to make a pale mixture; mix the chocolate and rum into the other half to make a dark mixture.

4 Pour about half of the pale mixture into the prepared tin, then all the dark mixture, and then the remaining pale mixture. Spiral a fork through the layers of mixture to create a marbled effect.

5 Bake the cake on the bottom shelf of the oven for 40–45 minutes, or until a skewer inserted in the centre comes out clean. Remove from the oven and allow to cool in the tin on a wire rack for about 10 minutes, then turn out onto the rack to cool completely.

6 Following the directions on the packet, soften the dark and white icing. Coat the cake with the dark glaze first, then allow to harden a little. Fill a piping (icing) bag with the white icing and make white lines on the dark glaze. Using a toothpick or small skewer, break up the white lines to form an attractive pattern on the cake.

⤚ When marbling a cake, don't overdo it or the effect will be spoiled. Just a few turns of the fork will be enough to create an attractive swirling pattern.

⤚ This cake tastes even better a day after baking; wrap in foil and allow the flavour to develop.

BLACK FOREST CHERRY CAKE

PASTRY BASE

125 g (4 oz) plain
    (all-purpose) flour
1/2 teaspoon baking powder
pinch salt
60 g (2 oz) butter, softened
2 tablespoons sugar
2 egg yolks, lightly beaten

CAKE

7 eggs
250 g (8 oz) sugar
60 g (2 oz) butter
150 g (5 oz) plain
    (all-purpose) flour
1/3 cup (40 g) cornflour (cornstarch)
1/3 cup (40 g) unsweetened cocoa
    powder
1 teaspoon baking powder

FILLING AND DECORATION

1 jar pitted sour (morello) cherries
    (about 800 g/28 oz)
5 g (1 1/2 teaspoons) powdered clear
    gelatin
pinch ground cloves
1 stick cinnamon
1/3 cup (100 g) sour cherry jam
1/4 cup (60 ml) Kirsch
3 cups (750 ml) cream,
    for whipping
few drops vanilla extract
dark chocolate, for grating

••• PREPARATION 1 hour 30 minutes
    plus chilling
••• COOKING About 45 minutes
••• SERVES 14

1 Preheat the oven to 170°C (340°F/ Gas 3). Line the base and side of a 25 cm (10 inch) springform cake tin with baking (parchment) paper.

2 To make the pastry, place all the ingredients in a mixing bowl. Combine using an electric mixer until the mixture forms a ball. Flatten the pastry into a disk, wrap in plastic wrap and chill for 30 minutes.

3 To make the cake, put the eggs and sugar in a heatproof bowl over a saucepan of gently simmering water. Whisk until the mixture is hot to the touch, pale and creamy. Remove bowl from pan and stir mixture until cold.

4 Melt the butter and allow to cool. Sift the flour, cornflour, cocoa and baking powder and fold into the egg mixture using a metal spoon. Fold in the butter.

5 Pour the mixture into the prepared tin, smooth the top and bake for 30 minutes. Remove from the oven and leave in the tin for a few minutes, then turn out onto a wire rack to cool. Reduce the oven temperature to 160°C (320°F/Gas 2–3). Slice the cake into 3 horizontal layers.

6 Roll out the chilled pastry and cut out a 25 cm (10 inch) circle of dough. Place the pastry base on a baking tray lined with baking (parchment) paper and prick several times with a fork. Bake for 10–12 minutes, or until golden brown. Remove from oven and allow to cool.

7 To make the filling, drain the jar of cherries, reserving the juice. Sprinkle the gelatin over a little cold water and allow to soak for about 10 minutes. Heat 250 ml (1 cup) cherry juice in a pan with the cloves and cinnamon stick. Remove the spices after a few minutes. Stir the gelatin into the hot juice to dissolve; cool.

8 Spread the jam over the pastry base. Place a cake layer on top. Drizzle with a little Kirsch, then spread with half of the thickened cherry juice. Place half the cherries on top. Beat the cream with the vanilla until thick and spreadable. Spread one-quarter of the cream over cherries.

9 Place the second cake layer on top. Drizzle with a little Kirsch and cover with the remaining thickened juice. Arrange cherries on top, reserving 14 of them for decoration. Spread another quarter of the cream over the cherries. Place the third cake layer on top; drizzle with Kirsch.

10 Spread cream on the side of the cake. Spoon the rest into a piping (icing) bag. Coarsely grate chocolate over the top and side of the cake. Pipe cream rosettes on top; place a reserved cherry on each one.

This all-time favourite is worth the effort it takes to make. If you're in a hurry, but still crave that combination of chocolate, cherries and cream, make the cake without the shortcrust pastry base. It will still taste delicious.

LOW-FAT BLACK FOREST CAKE

4½ tablespoons (55 g)
    unsweetened cocoa powder
4 tablespoons (50 g) plain (all-
    purpose) flour, sifted
1 cup (220 g) sugar, plus
    1½ tablespoons extra
pinch salt
8 large eggwhites
1 teaspoon cream of tartar
1½ teaspoons vanilla extract

•➤• PREPARATION 30 minutes
•➤• COOKING 25 minutes
•➤• SERVES 8

⁓ If your cake is going to be kept in the refrigerator for more than a couple of hours, construct a loose tent of foil around it. This will prevent it from absorbing the odours of any other foods.

FILLING

1½ tablespoons water
1 teaspoon powdered clear gelatin
1 tablespoon soft brown sugar
2 teaspoons cornflour (cornstarch)
½ teaspoon grated lemon zest
425 g (15 oz) can water-packed pitted sour
    (morello) cherries, drained (reserve
    the juice)
⅓ cup (80 ml) cream, for whipping
1 tablespoon icing (confectioners') sugar
⅓ cup (80 ml) low-fat evaporated milk,
    chilled
1 teaspoon lemon juice

1 Preheat oven to 190°C (375°F/Gas 5). Line the bases of two 20 cm (8 inch) cake tins with baking (parchment) paper.

2 Onto a plate, sift together the cocoa, flour, 1 cup sugar and the salt.

3 In a large bowl using an electric mixer, beat the eggwhites on medium speed until foamy. Add the cream of tartar and remaining sugar and beat until the whites

*This impressive dessert cake is worth the effort;
you'll find yourself asking for seconds of this
low-fat version of the classic recipe.*

hold soft peaks. Increase the speed to medium–high, then add 1 teaspoon vanilla and beat for a further minute. The whites should be soft and firm, not stiff and dry.

4 With a spatula, gently fold the cocoa mixture into the eggwhites, one-third at a time, then carefully divide the mixture between the tins. Bake for 20–25 minutes, or until the mixture begins to pull away from the sides of the tins and a skewer inserted in the centres comes out clean.

5 Remove from the oven. Invert onto a wire rack and allow to cool upside down in the tins. When the cakes are at room temperature, loosen their sides with a metal spatula. Turn them out on a work surface and remove the paper.

6 To prepare the filling, put the water and gelatin in a small bowl and let stand over a saucepan of hot water for 5 minutes to soften. Place over very low heat and cook, stirring, for about 3 minutes, or until the gelatin dissolves. Set aside.

7 In another small saucepan, combine the brown sugar, cornflour and lemon

zest. Slowly whisk in 1/2 cup (125 ml) of the reserved cherry juice until smooth. Bring the mixture to a boil over medium heat, then add most of the cherries (reserving some for decoration) and mix well. Set aside.

8 In a small bowl using an electric mixer, beat the cream on high speed until it holds soft peaks. Add the icing sugar and the remaining vanilla and beat until the cream holds stiff peaks.

9 In another small bowl, combine the evaporated milk and lemon juice and beat with clean beaters on high speed until very stiff. Beat in the cooled gelatin mixture and fold in the whipped cream.

10 To assemble, place a cake layer on a cake plate. Top with the cherry mixture, spreading it to the edge. Gently spread 1 cup whipped cream mixture over the cherry mixture. Place the second cake layer on the top. Using a large piping (icing) bag fitted with a star tip, pipe rosettes of the remaining cream mixture around the edge and in the centre of the cake. Decorate with the reserved cherries. Refrigerate until ready to serve.

CHOCOLATE MINT CAKE

125 g (4 oz) unsalted butter
150 g (5 oz) dark chocolate
handful finely chopped fresh mint
    or chocolate mint leaves (or
    1 teaspoon peppermint extract)
6 large eggs, separated
pinch salt
⅓ cup (80 g) caster (superfine)
    sugar
1½ cups (150 g) almond meal
    (ground almonds)
strawberries, blackberries,
    blueberries and/or raspberries,
    to serve
icing (confectioners') sugar,
    for dusting
whipped cream, to serve

•• PREPARATION 25 minutes
•• COOKING 40 minutes
•• SERVES 8

Chocolate mint has the taste
and aroma of an after-dinner
chocolate mint. Use in chocolate
desserts such as mousse and
ice-cream, or as a garnish.

1 Preheat the oven to 170°C (340°F/Gas 3).
Grease a 20 cm (8 inch) springform cake tin;
line the base with baking (parchment) paper.

2 Break the chocolate into pieces. Melt with
the butter in a medium heatproof bowl over
a saucepan of barely simmering water, stirring
occasionally. Remove from the heat; cool slightly.
Stir in the mint leaves.

3 In a medium bowl using an electric mixer,
beat the eggwhites and salt until soft peaks form.
Gradually add the sugar, whisking well after each
addition until just dissolved.

4 Beat the egg yolks in a large bowl, then stir in
the almond meal. Pour in the cooled chocolate
mixture; mix well. Using a metal spoon, fold in
2 large spoonfuls of eggwhite to lighten mixture,
then carefully and quickly fold in the remainder.

5 Pour the mixture into the prepared tin. Bake
for 35–40 minutes, or until the cake is well risen
and just firm to the touch. Cool in the tin on a
wire rack for 15 minutes, then turn out onto the
rack to cool completely. The cake will sink
slightly in the centre.

6 Decorate cooled cake with fresh berries; dust
with sifted icing sugar. Serve with whipped cream.

SULTANA–PECAN CHOCOLATE CAKE

Quick to prepare yet utterly delicious — this is a great standby recipe that can be eaten as is, or dressed up for a special occasion.

This is an easygoing recipe that lends itself to experimentation with different nuts and liqueurs.

¼ cup (50 g) pecans, finely chopped

¼ cup (50 g) sultanas (golden raisins)

2 tablespoons rum, brandy or other liqueur of your choice

200 g (7 oz) dark chocolate, chopped

175 g (6 oz) butter, chopped

¼ cup (55 g) caster (superfine) sugar

3 large eggs

1 tablespoon cornflour (cornstarch) or plain (all-purpose) flour

icing (confectioners') sugar or unsweetened cocoa powder, sifted, for dusting

<small>

•→ PREPARATION 15 minutes, plus soaking

•→ COOKING 50 minutes

•→ SERVES 10

</small>

1 In a small bowl, combine the pecans, sultanas and rum or brandy, cover and let soak for at least 30 minutes, or overnight.

2 Preheat the oven to 160°C (320°F/Gas 2–3). Grease a 22–23 cm (8–9 inch) cake tin and line it with baking (parchment) paper.

3 Melt the chocolate and butter together in a saucepan over low heat or in the microwave, stirring occasionally. Cool slightly.

4 Beat the sugar and eggs using an electric mixer on medium speed for about 5 minutes, or until pale and increased in volume. On low speed, beat in the chocolate and butter.

5 With a large metal spoon, fold in the cornflour, flour, pecans, sultanas and their soaking liquid until well combined, then pour into the prepared tin. The mixture will be quite runny.

6 Bake for about 50 minutes, or until risen, dry on the surface but still slightly soft in the middle — a skewer inserted in the centre should come out with a few moist crumbs sticking to it. (It is better to undercook the cake than to overcook it.) If the cake starts to brown too much towards the end of the cooking time, cover it loosely with foil.

7 Cool in the tin on a wire rack. (It will sink in the middle.) Serve warm or cold. It will keep in an airtight container for several days. In hot weather, cover it with plastic wrap and store in the refrigerator. Dust with icing sugar or cocoa powder and serve.

Cakes that contain a high percentage of chocolate, such as this one, will not test 'clean' when a skewer is inserted into them. Instead, test until the skewer comes out with just a few fudgy crumbs attached to it, then remove the cake from the oven. This will ensure a moist, dense texture. The cake will firm up further as it cools.

For variety, try different combinations of ingredients. One option is to omit the pecans and sultanas, and add the rum or brandy with the chocolate mixture. Another is to replace the flour with 1 cup (100 g) nut meal (ground nuts), such as almond or hazelnut. Or, for a chocolate–orange cake, replace the rum or brandy with orange liqueur such as Cointreau (or orange juice) and add 1–2 teaspoons finely grated orange zest with the chocolate mixture.

CHOCOLATE TORTE

CHOCOLATE SPONGE CAKE

200 g (7 oz) dark chocolate
  (at least 60 per cent cocoa),
  chopped
100 g (3½ oz) butter, chopped
6 very large eggs
150 g (5 oz) sugar
4 tablespoons brandy
1 cup (100 g) almond meal
  (ground almonds)
50 g (1¾ oz) cornflour
  (cornstarch)

CHOCOLATE CREAM

300 g (10 oz) dark chocolate
  (at least 60 per cent cocoa), chopped
250 g (8 oz) butter, softened
300 ml (10 fl oz) pouring cream
190 g (6½ oz) icing (confectioners') sugar
4 tablespoons brandy

GARNISH

chocolate leaves (ready-made or
  homemade; see page 13)
unsweetened cocoa powder, for dusting

⋅➤⋅ **PREPARATION** 40 minutes
⋅➤⋅ **COOKING** About 1 hour
⋅➤⋅ **SERVES** 12

A dream for chocolate fans! If you use chocolate with the highest possible cocoa content, the cream will be beautifully dark and have an intense chocolate taste.

1 Preheat the oven to 180°C (350°F/ Gas 4). Grease a 25 cm (10 inch) springform cake tin.

2 To make the sponge cake, melt the chocolate in a heatproof bowl set over a saucepan of barely simmering water. Add the butter and stir until melted. Remove from the heat and allow to cool a little. In a large bowl using an electric mixer, beat the eggs and sugar to a thick, pale cream;

then add the brandy 1 tablespoonful at a time. Fold in the chocolate, almond meal and cornflour. Pour the mixture into the prepared tin and bake in the centre of the oven for 1 hour. Cool in the tin on a wire rack for 10 minutes, then turn out onto the rack and leave to cool for at least 2 hours.

3 To make the chocolate cream icing, heat the cream in a small saucepan until just below boiling point. Remove from the heat, add the chocolate and stir until melted. Allow to cool, then refrigerate for at least 1 hour.

4 Stir together the butter and icing sugar until creamy. Beat the chocolate cream with an electric mixer until creamy, then stir into the butter mixture 1 tablespoonful at a time.

5 Cut the cake in half horizontally. Drizzle the cut surfaces with brandy. Spread the lower half of the cake with half of the chocolate cream, and cover with the top of the cake. Spread the top and side of the cake with the remaining chocolate cream. Garnish the edge of the cake with chocolate leaves and dust the centre with cocoa powder.

SECRET INGREDIENT CHOCOLATE CAKE

125 g (4 oz) dark chocolate
   (at least 70 per cent cocoa),
   broken into pieces
400 g (14 oz) can red kidney beans
   or black beans, rinsed and
   drained
2 large eggs, lightly beaten
½ cup (110 g) sugar
¼ teaspoon baking powder
2 teaspoons vanilla extract
icing (confectioners') sugar,
   for dusting
fresh raspberries or sliced
   strawberries, to serve
reduced-fat ricotta, to serve
   (optional)

⁙ PREPARATION 20 minutes
⁙ COOKING 45 minutes
⁙ SERVES 8

No one will guess the surprise ingredient in this fudgy, intensely chocolatey cake. You can't taste the beans, but their fibre and protein help to balance the carbohydrate and lower the glycaemic index of the cake.

1 Preheat the oven to 180°C (350°F/Gas 4). Grease a 20 cm (8 inch) cake tin and line the base with baking (parchment) paper.

2 Melt the chocolate in a heatproof bowl over a saucepan of simmering water. Stir until smooth.

3 Process the beans to a purée in a food processor or blender. Add the eggs, sugar, baking powder and vanilla. Process until smooth and creamy, stopping several times to scrape down the side of the bowl. Add the melted chocolate and pulse several times, or until thoroughly blended.

4 Spoon the mixture into the prepared tin and bake for 35–45 minutes, until the top springs back when touched lightly. (The cake will look cracked.) Cool in the tin on a wire rack for 5 minutes, then loosen the edges with a knife, invert the cake onto the rack and peel off the paper. Leave to cool a little.

5 Dust with icing sugar. Serve slightly warm or at room temperature for the fudgiest texture, accompanied by berries. Serve with ricotta on the side, if desired.

CHOCOLATE APRICOT CAKE

*T*he richness of chocolate and the tang of apricots go
well together. This Austrian cake contains apricots
in the form of both jam and liqueur.

- **PREPARATION** 40 minutes
- **COOKING** 45 minutes
- **SERVES** 10–12

dry breadcrumbs, for sprinkling
150 g (5 oz) dark chocolate,
    chopped
150 g (5 oz) butter, softened
150 g (5 oz) sugar
4 eggs, separated
100 g (3½ oz) self-raising flour
pinch salt
1 cup (100 g) almond meal
    (ground almonds)

TOPPING

½ cup (125 ml) apricot or orange
    liqueur
3 tablespoons apricot jam
¼ cup (60 ml) pouring cream
200 g (7 oz) milk chocolate, finely
    chopped
60 g (2 oz) butter, chopped

1 Preheat the oven to 180°C (350°F/Gas 4). Grease a 24 cm (9½ inch) springform cake tin and sprinkle the breadcrumbs over the base, tapping out any excess. Melt the chocolate in a heatproof bowl over a saucepan of simmering water. Allow to cool for about 10 minutes.

2 Beat the butter and half of the sugar until light and creamy. Stir the egg yolks, melted chocolate mixture and flour gradually into the butter mixture.

3 Beat the eggwhites and salt using an electric mixer until stiff, then gradually beat in the remaining sugar.

4 Fold the beaten eggwhites and the almond meal into the chocolate mixture. Pour into the prepared tin, smooth the surface and bake in the centre of the oven for about 45 minutes. Cool in the tin on a wire rack for 10 minutes, then turn out onto the rack to cool completely.

5 Prick the top of the cake all over with a fork and drizzle with liqueur. Warm the jam and press through a sieve. Coat the cake all over with a thin layer of jam.

6 Heat the cream in a small saucepan until just below boiling; remove from the heat. Melt the chocolate in the cream, stirring, then stir in the butter. Leave to cool for about 5 minutes, and then spread the topping all over the cake.

For the topping, heat the cream until just about to boil, then remove the pan from the stove; melt the chopped chocolate in the hot cream.

Cover the cake with a layer of apricot jam, then spread it evenly with chocolate icing.

RICH CHOCOLATE TORTE

175 g (6 oz) good-quality dark
chocolate (at least 70 per cent
cocoa), broken into pieces
85 g (3 oz) unsalted butter
4 eggs
½ cup (95 g) lightly packed soft
brown sugar
35 g (1 oz) plain (all-purpose) flour
cape gooseberries (physalis),
papery skins folded back,
to decorate (optional)
icing (confectioners') sugar,
for dusting
unsweetened cocoa powder,
for dusting

• PREPARATION 20 minutes
• COOKING 20 minutes
• SERVES 10

Good-quality dark chocolate makes this cake beautifully moist and rich — just a small slice will satisfy any sweet tooth.

1 Preheat oven to 180°C (350°F/Gas 4). Grease a 24 cm (9½ inch) springform cake tin and line the base and side with baking (parchment) paper. Grease the paper.

2 Put the chocolate and butter in a heatproof bowl set over a saucepan of barely simmering water, making sure the water does not touch the base of the bowl. Leave to melt, then remove from the heat and stir until smooth.

3 Meanwhile, beat the eggs and brown sugar in a large bowl using an electric mixer until the mixture has increased in volume and leaves a trail on the surface when the beaters are lifted out. (If using a hand whisk or rotary beater, set the bowl over a pan of almost-boiling water, making sure the water is not touching the base of the bowl.)

4 Add the chocolate mixture to the egg mixture and fold in with a large metal spoon. Gradually sift the flour over the top, folding in until it is just combined.

5 Spoon the mixture into the prepared tin, gently spreading it level. Bake for 15–20 minutes, or until the top of the cake feels just firm to the touch. Cool in the tin on a wire rack.

6 Remove the cake from the tin and peel away the paper. Cut into thin wedges for serving, decorating each with a cape gooseberry, if using, and dusting the cake and serving plate with sifted icing sugar and cocoa. The cake can be kept in the refrigerator for 2–3 days.

When slicing a cake that contains a lot of chocolate, such as this one, use a long knife, dip it into hot water and wipe the blade. This will produce a neat, clean cut. Repeat before each cut.

CHOCOLATE RING CAKE

250 g (8 oz) butter
160 g (5½ oz) sugar
4 eggs, separated
500 g (1 lb) plain (all-purpose)
    flour
2 teaspoons baking powder
½ cup (125 ml) milk
⅓ cup (60 g/2 oz) choc chips
    or finely chopped chocolate
60 g (2 oz) dark chocolate, melted,
    for icing

•‣· PREPARATION 15 minutes
•‣· COOKING About 65 minutes
•‣· SERVES 12

1 Preheat the oven to 180°C (350°F/ Gas 4). Grease a 24 cm (9½ inch) fluted ring or bundt tin and dust with flour, shaking out any excess.

2 Beat the butter and sugar using an electric mixer until the mixture is light and creamy and the sugar has dissolved. Stir in the egg yolks.

3 Sift the flour and baking powder. Add to the butter mixture in batches, alternating with the milk. Mix until all the ingredients are combined.

4 Beat the eggwhites until stiff and fold into the mixture with a spatula or large metal spoon. Fold in the chocolate chips.

5 Pour the mixture into the prepared tin. Smooth the top with a spatula.

6 Bake for 65 minutes in the centre of the oven, or until cooked when tested with a skewer.

7 Cool in the tin on a wire rack for 10 minutes, then turn out onto the rack to cool completely.

8 When the cake has cooled, cover with melted chocolate.

✎ Remove any cold ingredients from the refrigerator 1 hour before beginning so that they will be at room temperature.

✎ For a Chocolate Walnut Cake, chop ⅔ cup (100 g) dark chocolate and ½ cup (60 g) walnuts and fold them into the basic mixture along with the eggwhites. Cook and cool as instructed above. Cover the cake with melted dark chocolate.

Dust the greased cake tin with flour, turning the tin to distribute it evenly. Tip out any excess.

Using a spatula, gently fold the beaten eggwhites into the batter.

Spoon the mixture into the prepared tin, spreading it to the edges, and smooth the top.

CHOCOLATE RING CAKE WITH RICOTTA TOPPING

A sweet prune purée enriches this chocolate cake. It's crowned with a creamy but low-fat Italian-style topping made of ricotta.

- ⅔ cup (160 g) chopped pitted prunes
- 150 ml (5 fl oz) boiling water
- 3 tablespoons unsalted butter, softened
- ¾ cup (140 g) lightly packed soft brown sugar
- 1 teaspoon vanilla extract
- 2 eggs, beaten
- 100 g (3½ oz) self-raising white flour
- 100 g (3½ oz) self-raising wholemeal (whole-wheat) flour
- 1 teaspoon baking powder
- ⅓ cup (40 g) unsweetened cocoa powder, plus extra for dusting

RICOTTA TOPPING

- 1 cup (250 g) ricotta
- ½ teaspoon vanilla extract
- 1 tablespoon icing (confectioners') sugar, or to taste, sifted

-•- PREPARATION 25 minutes plus 30 minutes soaking
-•- COOKING 25 minutes
-•- SERVES 10

Serve this cake with coffee or for dessert. Try it with some fresh berries on the side.

1 Combine the prunes and boiling water in a bowl. Cover and set aside to soak for 30 minutes.

2 Preheat the oven to 180°C (350°F/ Gas 4). Grease a 20 cm (8 inch) ring tin.

3 Beat the butter using an electric mixer until light and creamy, then gradually beat in the brown sugar. Purée the prunes and soaking liquid in a blender until smooth, then add to the butter and sugar mixture and the vanilla. Mix well. Gradually beat in the eggs.

4 Sift the flours, baking powder and cocoa over the mixture, tipping in any bran left in the sieve. Fold in the dry ingredients until evenly combined. The

mixture should have a soft dropping consistency; add a little water if necessary. Spoon the mixture into the prepared tin, spreading it evenly.

5 Bake for about 25 minutes, or until well risen, slightly cracked on top and firm to the touch. Cool in the tin on a wire rack for 10 minutes, then run a knife around the inside of the tin to loosen the cake and turn it out onto the rack to cool completely. (The cake, minus the icing, can be kept in an airtight container for 3 days. Ice it just before serving.)

6 To make the icing, press the ricotta through a sieve into a bowl. Add the vanilla and icing sugar, and beat until smooth.

7 Place the cake on a serving plate and spoon the ricotta icing evenly around the top. Use a knife to swirl the icing slightly, taking it a little way down the side of the cake. Dust a little cocoa over the icing. Serve the cake as soon as possible.

To soften butter, leave it at room temperature for 45–60 minutes. If you're in a hurry, microwave the whole block of butter on a plate on the lowest setting in 30-second bursts. Take care not to overdo it; the butter should be soft but not at all melted, and still holding its shape.

RICH AND MOIST CHOCOLATE BUNDT CAKE

dry breadcrumbs, for dusting

300 g (10 oz) plain (all-purpose)
  flour

½ cup (60 g) unsweetened cocoa
  powder

1 teaspoon baking powder

½ teaspoon bicarbonate of soda
  (baking soda)

½ teaspoon salt

125 g (4 oz) unsalted butter,
  softened

300 g (10 oz) firmly packed dark
  brown sugar

4 large eggs

¾ cup (185 g) sour cream

2 teaspoons vanilla extract

•⋯ PREPARATION 15 minutes
•⋯ COOKING 50 minutes
•⋯ SERVES 12

Sour cream keeps this cake
rich and moist. You can make the
cake up to 1 month ahead. Wrap
the cooled cake in plastic and foil,
then store in the freezer. Bring to
room temperature before serving.

1 Preheat the oven to 180°C (350°F/Gas 4).
Grease a 25 cm (10 inch) ring or bundt tin.
Dust with breadcrumbs, tilting the tin so that
it is covered evenly. Tip out any excess.

2 In a medium bowl, stir together the flour,
cocoa, baking powder, bicarbonate of soda
and salt.

3 In a large bowl, beat the butter and sugar using
an electric mixer on medium speed for about
5 minutes, or until well blended. Beat in the eggs
one at a time, beating well after each addition.

4 Decrease the mixer speed to low and beat in
the flour mixture in three batches, alternating
with the sour cream. Beat in the vanilla.

5 Spoon into the prepared tin and bake for
40–50 minutes, or until a skewer inserted in
the centre comes out with only a few moist
crumbs attached. Cool in the tin on a wire rack
for 10 minutes, then turn out onto the rack to
cool completely.

Red chocolate bundt cake

*B*eetroot is quite sweet. When cooked and puréed,
it complements the bittersweet taste of dark chocolate
and gives chocolate cakes an attractive reddish hue.

250 g (8 oz) unsalted butter,
  softened
1⅓ cups (300 g) firmly packed
  dark brown sugar
3 eggs
125 g (4 oz) dark chocolate
2 cups (410 g) puréed cooked
  beetroot (beets)
1 teaspoon vanilla extract
300 g (10 oz) plain (all-purpose
  flour
2 teaspoons bicarbonate of soda
  (baking soda)
⅓ cup (40 g) unsweetened cocoa
  powder (optional; add if you
  want a richer flavour)
¼ teaspoon salt
icing (confectioners') sugar, for
  dusting

- PREPARATION 15 minutes
- COOKING 50 minutes
- SERVES 16

1 Preheat the oven to 190°C (375°F/Gas 5).
Grease a 25 cm (10 inch) fluted tube or bundt tin.
Dust with flour, tilting the tin so that it is covered
evenly. Tip out any excess.

2 In a medium bowl, cream 185 g (6 oz) butter
and the brown sugar. Add the eggs, one at a
time, beating well after each addition.

3 Melt the chocolate with the remaining butter
in a small microwavable bowl on medium power
for 3 minutes, stopping to stir every minute until
smooth. Cool slightly. Blend the chocolate
mixture, beetroot and vanilla into the creamed
mixture (the mixture will appear separated).

4 Sift the flour, bicarbonate of soda, cocoa and
salt over the creamed mixture. Mix well.

5 Pour into the tin and bake for 45–55 minutes, or
until a skewer inserted in the centre comes out
clean. Cool in the tin on a wire rack for 10 minutes,
then turn out onto the rack to cool completely.
Dust with icing sugar just before serving.

LAYER CAKE WITH CHOCOLATE GLAZE

*T*his cake is baked layer by layer. The rings that appear when it is sliced resemble tree rings, giving the cake its German name, *Baumkuchen*.

dry breadcrumbs, for dusting
5 eggs, separated
100 g (3½ oz) sugar
1 teaspoon vanilla extract
grated zest of 1 lemon
100 g (3½ oz) butter
50 g (1¾ oz) plain (all-purpose) flour
50 g (1¾ oz) cornflour (cornstarch)

CHOCOLATE GLAZE

150 g (5 oz) dark chocolate, broken into pieces
200 g (7 oz) sugar
1 tablespoon rum (optional)
1 tablespoon butter, if needed

⋯ **PREPARATION** 1 hour
⋯ **COOKING** About 30 minutes
⋯ **MAKES** 16 large slices or 40 small choc-dipped bites

1 Preheat the oven to 150°C (300°F/ Gas 2). Grease a 24 cm (9½ inch) springform cake tin. Sprinkle breadcrumbs over the base, tipping out any excess.

2 Using an electric mixer, beat the egg yolks with the sugar, vanilla and lemon zest until the sugar is completely dissolved. Add the butter and beat until the mixture is thick and creamy.

3 Sift the flour and cornflour over the egg yolk mixture and beat in thoroughly to form a batter. In a separate bowl and using clean, dry beaters, beat the egg-whites until stiff. Fold into the batter.

4 Place 2–3 tablespoons batter on the base of the prepared tin and spread smoothly using a broad pastry brush or a dough scraper. Bake for 3–5 minutes.

5 When the layer is browned, spread a second layer of batter onto the first. Bake as before, this time sliding an empty baking tray into the oven underneath the cake to reduce the heat on the bottom of the cake.

6 Continue in the same manner until all the batter is used. Remove from the oven, leave to cool, then remove from the tin.

7 The cake can be glazed whole, or in triangular slices, or the slices cut into smaller pieces then glazed. To make the glaze, melt the chocolate in a heat-proof bowl over a saucepan of barely simmering water. Stir until smooth. Add ½ cup (125 ml) water, the sugar and the rum, if using. Stir constantly until smooth and evenly coloured.

8 Leave the glaze to cool a little. If the mixture becomes too hard, add the butter and gently warm the mixture again to make the glaze smoother and more liquid. Spread over the cake, or dip the slices or pieces in the glaze. Leave to set on a wire rack set over a baking tray to catch any drips.

When preparing the cake you will need time, peace and quiet, as the individual layers of batter must be added with care, and watched constantly while they cook.

VIENNESE SACHERTORTE

150 g (5 oz) dark chocolate,
  broken into pieces
150 g (5 oz) butter
1¼ cups (150 g) icing
  (confectioners') sugar
few drops vanilla extract
6 eggs, separated
125 g (4 oz) plain (all-purpose)
  flour
¼ teaspoon baking powder
3–4 tablespoons apricot jam
200 g (7 oz) dark chocolate

- PREPARATION 30 minutes
- COOKING 70 minutes
- SERVES 8

Use the best-quality dark chocolate you can afford for this cake. Store the cake for a day, if possible, to allow the full depth of flavour to develop.

1 Preheat the oven to 150°C (300°F/Gas 2). Line the base of a 23 cm (9 inch) springform cake tin with baking (parchment) paper.

2 Melt the chocolate in heatproof bowl set over a saucepan of simmering water. Using an electric mixer on medium speed, beat the chocolate, butter, icing sugar, vanilla and egg yolks until well combined. Sift the flour and baking powder over the mixture and stir in. Beat the eggwhites in a separate bowl using clean, dry beaters until stiff. Fold into the mixture with a metal spoon.

3 Spoon the mixture into the prepared tin and smooth the top, building the mixture up a little higher towards the edge. Bake for 60–70 minutes. Remove from the oven and let stand in the tin for 5 minutes, then remove the outer ring of the tin. Cover the cake with baking paper, weigh down with a small board and leave to cool completely. Turn onto a wire rack and remove the base of the tin.

4 Sieve the jam into a small saucepan, add a little water and heat gently. Spread evenly over the cake and allow to set. Melt the chocolate in a bowl set over simmering water and spread over the cake. To prevent cracking, lift the cake onto a serving plate before the chocolate hardens.

CHOCOLATE–PECAN TORTE

1½ cups (165 g) pecans
1 cup (220 g) sugar
170 g (6½ oz) dark chocolate
    (at least 60 per cent cocoa)
6 eggs, separated, at room
    temperature
¼ cup (30 g) unsweetened cocoa
    powder
⅓ cup (80 ml) orange juice
1 teaspoon grated orange zest
icing (confectioners') sugar
    (optional)
orange segments (optional)

- PREPARATION 15 minutes
- COOKING 40 minutes
- SERVES 16

This rich cake tastes even better the day after baking. Store, covered, for 1 day, or freeze any leftovers for future treats.

1 Preheat the oven to 180°C (350°F/Gas 4). Lightly grease a 25 cm (10 inch) springform cake tin. Pulse the pecans with half the sugar in a food processor until finely ground. Add the chocolate, then pulse until ground. Set aside.

2 In a large bowl, beat the eggwhites with an electric beater on high speed until foamy. Continue to beat, gradually adding the remaining sugar, until the eggwhites are stiff and shiny.

3 In another bowl, beat the egg yolks with the same beaters for about 4 minutes, or until thick. Add the cocoa, orange juice and zest, then beat until well blended. Fold in the pecan mixture. Stir in a quarter of the eggwhites, then fold in the rest in two batches. Spoon into the tin and bake for about 40 minutes, or until a skewer inserted in the centre comes out clean.

4 Cool completely in the tin on a wire rack. Run a knife around the inside of the tin, then release the side. Sprinkle the torte with icing sugar and top with orange segments, if desired.

CAPPUCCINO CHIFFON CAKE

300 g (10 oz) plain
(all-purpose) flour
1½ cups (345 g) caster (superfine)
sugar
1 tablespoon baking powder
1 teaspoon ground cinnamon
½ cup (125 ml) walnut oil
2 large eggs, separated, plus
4 large eggwhites
¾ cup (180 ml) brewed espresso
coffee, at room temperature
2 tablespoons unsweetened cocoa
powder
1 teaspoon vanilla extract
½ teaspoon cream of tartar
2 tablespoons icing
(confectioners') sugar

┄•┄ PREPARATION 15 minutes
┄•┄ COOKING 45 minutes
┄•┄ SERVES 16

1 Preheat the oven to 160°C (320°F/Gas 2–3).

2 In a medium bowl, stir together the flour, sugar, baking powder and cinnamon. Whisk the oil, egg yolks, coffee, cocoa and vanilla together in a large bowl until smooth. Fold flour mixture into the egg mixture until well combined.

3 Beat all the eggwhites in a medium bowl using an electric mixer until frothy. Beat in the cream of tartar and continue beating until stiff peaks form. Gently fold the eggwhites into the mixture.

4 Spoon the mixture into an ungreased 25 cm (10 inch) ring tin and smooth the top. Bake for about 45 minutes, or until a skewer inserted in the centre comes out clean.

5 Invert the tin onto a wire rack and allow the cake to cool. (Cooling this cake the right way up will cause it to sink.) Run a knife between the cake and the side of the tin and turn the cake onto a serving plate. Dust with icing sugar.

⌇ Walnut oil has a strong flavour. Replace it with extra-light olive oil, if preferred.

Very easy to make, this sweet treat is lower in fat than most. It has a fine, delicate texture and a rich coffee flavour.

FALLEN CHOCOLATE SOUFFLÉ CAKE

¾ cup (170 g) caster (superfine)
  sugar
½ cup (60 g) unsweetened cocoa
  powder
3 tablespoons dark chocolate
  chips
1½ teaspoons vanilla extract
1 large egg, separated, plus 4 large
  eggwhites
30 g (1 oz) plain (all-purpose) flour
¼ cup (25 g) wheatgerm, toasted
¼ teaspoon cream of tartar

500 g (1 lb) fresh or thawed frozen
  strawberries, plus extra fresh
  berries to decorate (optional)
⅓ cup (80 ml) orange juice
3 cups (750 g) vanilla frozen
  yogurt

⁂ PREPARATION 15 minutes
⁂ COOKING 25 minutes
⁂ SERVES 12

*A fallen cake is usually bad news, but this
rich-tasting one is a spectacular success,
especially when served with strawberry sauce.*

1 Preheat the oven to 190°C (375°F/Gas 5). Line a 23 cm (9 inch) springform cake tin with baking (parchment) paper and coat lightly with non-stick cooking spray.

2 In a saucepan, stir ½ cup (115 g) sugar, the cocoa and ¼ cup (60 ml) cold water until smooth. Add chocolate chips and cook over low heat, stirring, until melted. Stir in 1 teaspoon vanilla. Cool to room temperature. Stir in the egg yolk, flour and wheatgerm.

3 Beat all of the eggwhites using an electric mixer until frothy. Add the cream of tartar and continue beating until soft peaks form. Add the remaining sugar, 1 tablespoon at a time, and beat until stiff peaks form.

4 Using a metal spoon, fold one-quarter of the eggwhites into the chocolate mixture to lighten it. Fold the chocolate mixture into the remaining eggwhites until just combined. Spoon the mixture into the prepared tin and bake for about 25 minutes, or until a skewer inserted in the centre comes out clean. Cool the cake in the tin on a wire rack.

5 Meanwhile, purée the strawberries, orange juice and remaining vanilla in a food processor.

6 Remove the side of the tin. Slice the cake and serve with the strawberry sauce and frozen yogurt.

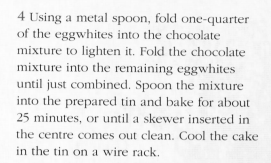

Need an excuse to indulge in this cake? Here are several to consider. This recipe uses dark chocolate and cocoa powder to give the cake a rich flavour. Dark chocolate is a good source of copper and it also provides useful amounts of iron, while cocoa powder contains five times as much iron as chocolate.

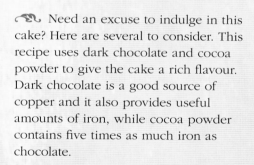

Chocolate, in particular the dark variety, contains valuable amounts of phenols, substances that work as an anti-oxidant and help to prevent harmful LDL cholesterol—the cholesterol that clogs arteries.

CHOCOLATE, PEAR AND WALNUT UPSIDE-DOWN CAKE

2 ripe but firm pears, peeled, cored and sliced
¾ cup (170 g) caster (superfine) sugar
2 eggs, lightly beaten
½ cup (125 g) natural (plain) yogurt
½ cup (125 ml) sunflower or vegetable oil
finely grated zest of 1 lime
150 g (5 oz) plain (all-purpose) flour
2 teaspoons baking powder
3 tablespoons unsweetened cocoa powder
⅓ cup (30 g) chopped walnuts
2 tablespoons icing (confectioners') sugar, sifted

·✦· PREPARATION 20 minutes
·✦· COOKING 50 minutes
·✦· SERVES 8

Any left-over cake can be covered with plastic wrap and kept in the fridge for 2–3 days.

1 Preheat the oven to 180°C (350°F/Gas 4). Grease a deep, loose-based 18 cm (7 inch) square cake tin or a deep 20 cm (8 inch) round cake tin. Line the base with baking (parchment) paper.

2 Arrange the pear slices over the bottom of the prepared cake tin.

3 In a large bowl, stir the caster sugar, eggs, yogurt, oil and lime zest in a large bowl until smooth and mixed thoroughly. Sift flour, baking powder and cocoa and fold into the egg mixture, alternating with the walnuts.

4 Spoon the mixture over the sliced pears and smooth the top. Bake for 50 minutes, or until golden brown and firm to the touch. Check after 30 minutes and cover with foil if the cake is browning too quickly.

5 Leave the cake in the tin for about 15 minutes, then turn out onto the rack of a grill (broiler) tray, pear side up. Peel off the paper. Preheat the grill. Dust cake thickly with icing sugar and place under the hot grill for 3–4 minutes, or until the sugar has melted and is golden. Leave to cool on the grill rack, then transfer to a plate to serve.

CHOCOLATE CHERRY CUPCAKES

150 g (5 oz) butter
½ cup (75 g) chopped dark chocolate
    (about 70 per cent cocoa)
½ cup (115 g) caster (superfine)
    sugar
2–3 drops vanilla extract
2 tablespoons red wine
4 eggs
280 g (10 oz) self-raising flour
1 tablespoon unsweetened cocoa
    powder
500 g (1 lb) cherries, pitted
melted white chocolate and whipped
    cream, to serve (optional)

PREPARATION 35 minutes
COOKING 25 minutes
MAKES 24

1 Preheat the oven to 180°C (350°F/Gas 4). Line two 12-hole standard (⅓ cup/80 ml) muffin tins or cupcake pans with paper cases, or use silicone moulds.

2 Melt the butter and chocolate in a heatproof bowl set over a saucepan of simmering water. Allow to cool.

3 Put the sugar, vanilla and red wine in a large bowl. Add melted chocolate mixture and stir well. Gradually stir in the eggs.

4 Sift in 250 g (8 oz) flour and the cocoa. Stir until combined. Place remaining flour on a deep plate. Make sure cherries are dry, then toss them in the flour. Fold the cherries into the cake mixture.

5 Spoon the mixture into the paper cases or moulds, filling them two-thirds full. Bake for 20–25 minutes, or until golden brown. Cool the cakes in the tin on a wire rack for 10 minutes, then lift them out the rack to cool completely. Drizzle lightly with melted white chocolate and serve with whipped cream. These cakes are best eaten on the day they are baked.

Buy loose cherries rather than pre-packaged ones. They should be plump, firm and shiny, with their flexible green stems still attached. Avoid sticky, damaged fruit. You can use a paper clip to remove cherry pits. Or use a cherry pitter, available from cookware stores.

WHITE CHOCOLATE CUPCAKES

125 g (4 oz) unsalted butter

125 g (4 oz) good-quality white
   chocolate, chopped

¼ cup (60 ml) milk

½ cup (115 g) caster (superfine)
   sugar

2 eggs, lightly beaten

225 g (7½ oz) self-raising flour

•◦ PREPARATION 15 minutes

•◦ COOKING 20 minutes

•◦ MAKES 12

1 Preheat the oven to 180°C (350°F/Gas 4).
Line a 12-hole standard (⅓ cup/80 ml) muffin
tin or cupcake pan with paper cases, or use
silicone moulds.

2 Combine the butter, chocolate and milk in a
medium saucepan over low heat. Stir until melted
and smooth. Remove from the heat and stir in
the sugar. Cool for 10 minutes.

3 Stir the eggs and flour into the chocolate
mixture. Spoon the mixture into the paper cases
or moulds and bake for 20 minutes, or until the
cakes spring back when lightly pressed.

4 Cool the cakes in the tin on a wire rack for
10 minutes, then lift them out onto the rack to
cool completely.

5 Ice with Vanilla Buttercream (page 248),
sprinkle with white chocolate curls (page 13)
and top with an almond coconut chocolate such
as Ferrero Raffaello. See more icing (frosting)
recipes and decoration ideas on page 248.

꙳ This easy melt-and-mix recipe is a cross
between a buttercake and a light mud cake.

CHOCOLATE CUPCAKES

125 g (4 oz) unsalted butter,
  softened
¾ cup (165 g) caster (superfine)
  sugar
2 large eggs, beaten
1 teaspoon vanilla extract
100 g (3½ oz) dark chocolate,
  melted
185 g (6 oz) plain
  (all-purpose) flour
2 teaspoons baking powder
1 tablespoon Dutch cocoa powder
¾ cup (180 ml) milk

CHOCOLATE BUTTERCREAM

125 g (4 oz) unsalted butter
1 cup (125 g) icing
  (confectioners') sugar, sifted
125 g (4 oz) dark chocolate,
  melted, cooled slightly

⤍ PREPARATION 10 minutes
⤍ COOKING 25 minutes
⤍ MAKES 12

1 Preheat the oven to 180°C (350/Gas 4).
Line a 12-hole standard (⅓ cup/80 ml) muffin
tin or cupcake pan with paper cases, or use
silicone moulds.

2 Using an electric mixer, beat the butter and
sugar until light and fluffy. Gradually beat in
the egg and vanilla. Add the melted chocolate
and beat until combined. Sift the flour, baking
powder and cocoa and fold through alternately
with the milk.

3 Spoon the mixture into the paper cases or
moulds and bake for 20–25 minutes, or until
a skewer inserted in the centre of a cupcake
comes out clean. Cool the cupcakes in the tin
for 10 minutes, then lift the cupcakes out onto
a wire rack to cool completely.

4 To make the chocolate buttercream, beat the
butter using an electric mixer until light and
creamy. Gradually beat in the icing sugar and
continue beating until the mixture is light and
fluffy. Add the melted chocolate and beat until
combined. Spread the icing over the cupcakes.
Allow to set before serving.

LAMINGTONS

2 cups (250 g) icing (confectioners') sugar
1/3 cup (40 g) unsweetened cocoa powder
1/4 cup (60 ml) milk
1/4 cup (60 ml) boiling water
two 20 cm (8 inch) square sponge cakes
1/3 cup (100 g) raspberry jam
2 cups (180 g) desiccated coconut

- PREPARATION 20 minutes
- COOKING Nil
- MAKES 16

1 To make the icing (frosting), sift the icing sugar and cocoa into a bowl. Add the milk and boiling water and stir until smooth.

2 Place one of the sponge cakes on a flat surface. Spread with the jam, top with the other sponge cake, then cut into 16 small squares.

3 Spread some of the coconut on a plate. Using two forks, roll a cake square in the chocolate icing until well coated, allowing any excess to drip off. Drop the cake into the coconut and roll with your fingers to coat well. Transfer to a wire rack to set. Coat the remaining cake squares in the same way, adding more coconut as needed. The lamingtons will keep in an airtight container for 3–4 days.

For speed and ease, we've used pre-made or bought sponge cakes. If using your own sponge cake recipe, bake the cakes in 2 shallow 20 cm (8 inch) square cake tins. Once cooked, leave in the tins for 5 minutes, then turn out onto a wire rack to cool. Cut into squares and coat as directed.

Even though it's not a traditional sponge cake for lamingtons, try the quick '2-4-6-8' cake, so named for the ratio of imperial measurements it uses. Lightly beat 2 eggs in a bowl, add 125 g (4 oz) softened butter, 175 g (6 oz) sugar and 225 g (8 oz) sifted self-raising flour. Mix with a wooden spoon. Pour into a 25 cm (10 inch) cake tin and bake at 200°C (400°F/Gas 6) for 30 minutes, or until a skewer inserted near the centre comes out clean. Cool, cut into squares and coat as directed.

This Australian classic is always popular.
Using day-old cake will make it easier
to slice and dip the squares.

CHOCOLATE FRIANDS

185 g (6 oz) unsalted butter

75 g (2½ oz) plain (all-purpose)
   flour

1½ cups (185 g) icing
   (confectioners') sugar

3 tablespoons unsweetened cocoa
   powder, plus extra for dusting

1 cup (100 g) almond meal
   (ground almonds)

5 eggwhites

→ **PREPARATION** 25 minutes

→ **COOKING** 20 minutes

→ **MAKES 12**

⟋ For white chocolate friands,
use 100 g (3½ oz) white chocolate,
finely chopped or grated, and
omit the cocoa powder.

1 Preheat the oven to 180°C (350°F/Gas 4).
Melt the butter in a small saucepan over low
heat. Set aside for about 15 minutes, or until cool.
Use a little of the melted butter to lightly grease
twelve ½ cup (125 ml) oval friand tins. Dust with
a little flour and shake out the excess.

2 Sift the flour, icing sugar and cocoa into a large
bowl. Stir in the almond meal and chopped or
grated chocolate, if using.

3 Lightly whisk the eggwhites in a separate bowl.
Add the eggwhites and melted butter to the dry
ingredients, stirring until completely combined.

4 Spoon the batter evenly into the friand moulds
until they are two-thirds to three-quarters full,
about 1 cm (½ inch) from the top. Bake for
about 20 minutes, until the tops have just started
to crack and a skewer inserted in the centre
comes out clean.

5 Remove from the oven, cool in the tins on a
wire rack for 5 minutes, then turn out onto the
rack to cool completely. When cool, dust with
cocoa and serve.

Bittersweet chocolate cheesecake

1 cup (100 g) chocolate wafer
  crumbs
½ cup (60 g) finely chopped
  toasted hazelnuts
85 g (3 oz) butter, melted
700 g (24 oz) cream cheese,
  softened
1 cup (220 g) sugar
350 g (12 oz) chocolate (at least
  70 per cent cocoa), melted and
  cooled
3 eggs, lightly beaten
1 cup (8 oz) sour cream
1½ teaspoons vanilla extract
½ teaspoon almond extract
pinch salt

Glaze

125 g (4 oz) chocolate (at least
  70 per cent cocoa)
¼ cup (60 ml) thickened (heavy/
  double) whipping cream
1 teaspoon vanilla extract
whipped cream and toasted
  chopped hazelnuts (optional)

- PREPARATION 15 minutes
- COOKING 65 minutes
- SERVES 16

1 Preheat the oven to 180°C (350°F/Gas 4). In a small bowl, combine the wafer crumbs and hazelnuts. Stir in the butter and press the mixture into the bottom of an ungreased 23 cm (9 inch) springform cake tin.

2 In a large bowl using an electric mixer, beat the cream cheese and sugar until smooth. Add the chocolate, then the eggs, and beat on low speed until just combined. Add the sour cream, extracts and salt, and beat until just blended. Pour over the crust.

3 Place the tin on a baking tray and bake for 60–65 minutes, or until the centre is almost set. Cool in the tin on a wire rack for 10 minutes. Carefully run a knife around the edge of the tin to loosen the cake. Cool for a further hour, then cover and refrigerate for 3 hours.

4 For the glaze, melt the chocolate with the cream, stirring until smooth. Remove from heat and stir in the vanilla.

5 Remove the side of the tin. Spread the glaze over the top of the cheesecake. Refrigerate overnight. Garnish with whipped cream and hazelnuts if desired. Store, covered, in the refrigerator for up to 3 days.

QUICK PEAR AND CHOCOLATE TART

butter, for greasing
1 sheet ready-rolled sweet
    shortcrust pastry, thawed
85 g (3 oz) dark chocolate, broken
    into pieces
⅓ cup (80 g) crème fraîche
    (see note)
2 tablespoons milk
825 g (29 oz) can pear halves,
    well drained
3 medium eggs

⁕ PREPARATION 10 minutes
⁕ COOKING 30 minutes
⁕ SERVES 6

1 Preheat the oven to 180°C (350°F/Gas 4).
Grease a 25 cm (10 inch) flan tin (tart pan).

2 Use the pastry to line the dish. Trim the edges.
Melt the chocolate in a small heatproof bowl set
over a saucepan of simmering water, or in the
microwave. Cool a little and add half the crème
fraîche and the milk. Stir until well combined.

3 Spread this mixture over the pastry then place
the drained pear halves evenly on the chocolate.
Mix the eggs with the rest of the crème fraîche
and pour over the tart. Bake for 30 minutes.

Crème fraîche is a slightly sour cultured
cream, available in many supermarkets and
delicatessens. To make your own, warm 1 cup
(250 ml) of thickened (heavy/double) whipping
cream, then add 1 tablespoon cultured buttermilk
and allow the mixture to thicken at room
temperature for 24 hours.

CHOCOLATE CARAMEL TART

*T*he combined flavours of chocolate, caramel and banana are simply delicious. This large cake is perfect for a crowd.

CHOCOLATE SPONGE CAKE

30 g (1 oz) butter
3 eggs
1 tablespoon boiling water
75 g (2½ oz) caster (superfine) sugar
pinch salt
50 g (1¾ oz) plain (all-purpose) flour
50 g (1¾ oz) cornflour (cornstarch)
15 g (½ oz) unsweetened cocoa powder
1 teaspoon baking powder
pinch ground cloves

TOPPING

400 g (14 oz) bananas
3 tablespoon lemon juice

CARAMEL CREAM

75 g (2½ oz) sugar
2 cups (500 ml) thickened (heavy/ double) whipping cream
4 tablespoons grated dark chocolate
whipped cream, chocolate ornaments (page 12) and extra cocoa powder, to garnish (optional)

⇢ PREPARATION 50 minutes
⇢ COOKING 30 minutes
⇢ SERVES 16–20

This recipe also works well as a small cake. Use a 20 cm (8 inch) cake tin and halve the ingredients.

1 Preheat the oven to 180°C (350°F/ Gas 4). Grease a 28 cm (11 inch) loose-based fluted flan tin (tart pan).

2 Melt the butter and allow to cool. Using an electric mixer, beat the eggs, boiling water, sugar and salt on the highest speed until thick, pale and creamy.

3 Combine the flour, cornflour, cocoa, baking powder and cloves. Sift the flour mixture onto the egg mixture, then fold in. Add the melted butter and fold in.

4 Pour into the prepared tin and bake in the centre of the oven for 25–30 minutes. Cool in the tin on a wire rack for 10 minutes, then turn out onto the rack and allow to cool for at least 1 hour.

5 To make the topping, peel the bananas and slice into a bowl. (If the bananas are thick, halve them lengthwise before slicing.) Add the lemon juice; this will prevent the bananas from turning brown.

6 To make the caramel cream, bring the sugar and 2 tablespoons water to a boil in a small saucepan. Stir with a small whisk over medium heat until the liquid looks glassy. Reduce the heat to low and cook, without stirring, until the syrup starts to caramelise. Remove from the heat. Carefully (as it will spatter), stir in 100 ml (3½ fl oz) cream, 1 tablespoon at a time. Leave the caramel cream to cool.

7 Place the sponge cake base on a cake plate. Arrange the banana slices on the cake. Beat the remaining cream until semi-stiff. Add the caramel cream and beat the mixture until completely stiff. Fold in the grated chocolate. Spread the caramel cream over the bananas and refrigerate until ready to cut. Before serving, garnish with dollops of cream and chocolate ornaments if desired, and dust with cocoa.

DECADENT CHOCOLATE TART WITH STRAWBERRIES

190 g (6½ oz) plain
   (all-purpose) flour
2 tablespoons icing
   (confectioners') sugar
100 g (3½ oz) butter, chilled
   and chopped
2½ tablespoons iced water
150 g (5 oz) dark chocolate,
   chopped
1¼ cups (300 ml) thickened
   (heavy/double) whipping
   cream
1 tablespoon soft brown sugar
2 eggs, lightly beaten
1 teaspoon vanilla extract
250 g (8 oz) strawberries
2 teaspoons icing (confectioners')
   sugar
whipped cream, to serve

⋯ PREPARATION 1 hour
⋯ COOKING 45 minutes
⋯ SERVES 8–10

This is the perfect dinner party dessert.
Cook it up to a day in advance; keep chilled,
but return to room temperature to serve.

1 Preheat the oven to 180°C (350°F/Gas 4).

2 To make the pastry, sift the flour and icing sugar into a bowl. Using your fingertips, rub in the butter until the mixture resembles fine breadcrumbs. Add the water and mix with a knife until the mixture starts to clump together. Gather the dough into a ball. Roll out on a sheet of baking (parchment) paper until large enough to fit a 22 cm (8½ inch) loose-based fluted flan tin (tart pan). If the rolling pin sticks, very lightly flour the surface of the pastry. Ease into the tin, and trim away the overhanging pastry. Place in the freezer for 10 minutes.

3 Line the pastry with baking paper and fill with dried rice or beans. Bake for 10 minutes, then remove paper and rice and bake for a further 10–15 minutes, until the pastry is dry and lightly golden. Cool completely. Store in an airtight container for up to 2 days.

4 To make the filling, combine the chocolate, cream and brown sugar in a medium bowl set over a saucepan of barely simmering water. Stand for about 5 minutes, until the chocolate is starting to melt, then stir until smooth. Remove

from the heat and cool slightly. Add the eggs and vanilla and stir until combined (be gentle, as you don't want air bubbles).

5 Stand the tin on a baking tray and fill the pastry case with the chocolate mixture. Bake for 20 minutes, or until just set. Transfer to a wire rack and cool to room temperature.

6 Meanwhile, wash, dry and hull the strawberries. Cut into quarters. Place in a bowl and sift the icing sugar over. Toss to combine and stand for 10 minutes, or until the berries are glossy and slightly syrupy. Spoon them over the chocolate filling. Cut the tart into wedges and serve with whipped cream.

To save time, make the pastry in a food processor. Combine the flour, icing sugar and butter in the bowl of the machine, and use the pulse button to process in short bursts until the mixture resembles breadcrumbs. Add the water and process, again in short bursts. The secret is to not overwork the dough. Tip out onto a work surface, gather the dough together and proceed with the recipe.

CHOCOLATE MOUSSE TART

215 g (7½ oz) digestive biscuit
  or chocolate graham cracker
  crumbs
1 large eggwhite
2 tablespoons honey
2 teaspoons (7 g) powdered clear
  gelatin
1 cup (230 g) caster (superfine)
  sugar
1 cup (125 g) unsweetened cocoa
  powder, plus extra for dusting
⅓ cup (80 ml) milk, warmed
1 teaspoon vanilla extract
1½ cups (375 ml) cream, for
  whipping
85 g (3 oz) dark chocolate, at room
  temperature, to decorate

⁌ PREPARATION 20 minutes
⁌ COOKING 10 minutes plus chilling
⁌ SERVES 8

Take care when softening
and dissolving gelatin, or it can
become lumpy. To soften, sprinkle
the powder evenly on top of the
liquid. Do not stir gelatin while it
is in the process of dissolving.

1 Preheat the oven to 180°C (350°F/Gas 4).
Lightly grease a 25 cm (10 inch) loose-based
non-stick fluted flan tin (tart pan).

2 Combine the crumbs, eggwhite and honey.
Press the crumb mixture into the bottom and
side of the prepared tin to make a crust. Bake for
10 minutes, then cool in the tin on a wire rack.

3 Put 3 tablespoons water in a saucepan and
sprinkle the gelatin over it. Stir over low heat for
about 2 minutes, or until the gelatin dissolves.
Remove from the heat.

4 Mix the sugar and cocoa in a large bowl. Stir
in the milk and vanilla until the cocoa dissolves.
Stir in the gelatin. Cool.

5 Whip the cream until stiff peaks form. Fold
three-quarters of the whipped cream into the
cooled cocoa mixture until blended. Pour into
the crust. Swirl the remaining whipped cream in
the centre. Refrigerate for 2 hours or overnight to
let the mousse set. Dust with cocoa and decorate
with chocolate curls.

6 To make chocolate curls, use room-temperature
chocolate. Draw the blade of a vegetable peeler
across it, pressing down firmly. Lift the curls into
place with a skewer or toothpick.

Chocolate and special occasions were made for each other. This spectacular tart is the perfect finish to a celebratory dinner.

CHOC–CHILLI TARTLETS

200 g (7 oz) dark chocolate
  (at least 60 per cent cocoa),
  chopped
150 g (5 oz) butter, softened
150 g (5 oz) sugar
5 eggs, separated
2 cups (200 g) almond meal
  (ground almonds)
2 pinches cayenne pepper
pinch salt
50 g (1¾ oz) plain (all-purpose)
  flour

TOPPING

2 small dried red chillies
100 g (3½ oz) pepitas (pumpkin
  seeds)
2 tablespoons soft brown sugar
200 g (7 oz) dark chocolate
30 g (1 oz) butter

- PREPARATION 40 minutes
- COOKING 25 minutes
- SERVES 10

1 Preheat the oven to 180°C (350°F/ Gas 4). Grease ten 13 cm (5 inch) flan tins (tart pans).

2 For the base, melt the chocolate in a heatproof bowl set over a saucepan of barely simmering water. Cool to room temperature.

3 Using an electric mixer, beat the butter and sugar until light and creamy. Add the egg yolks one by one, beating after each addition until light and fluffy. Mix in the almond meal, chocolate and cayenne pepper.

4 Beat the eggwhites with the salt until stiff. Fold the beaten eggwhites and the flour into the chocolate mixture. Divide the mixture evenly among the prepared tins and smooth the surface. Bake in the centre of the oven for about 25 minutes, then remove from the oven and leave to cool in the tins on a wire rack.

5 For the topping, remove the chilli stalks. Remove the seeds (or if you prefer more heat, leave them in). Chop the chillies finely.

6 Roast the chillies and the pepitas in a dry frying pan. Add the brown sugar and stir over low heat until melted. Pour the mixture onto a plate, separating the seeds as much as possible, and leave to cool. If the seeds stick to each other, separate them by hand.

7 Chop the chocolate finely and melt in a heatproof bowl set over a saucepan of barely simmering water. Chop the butter into small pieces. Add to the chocolate and stir to melt.

8 Remove the tartlets from the tins and coat with the chocolate mixture. Sprinkle immediately with the pepitas, and leave to harden.

When caramelising the pepitas, use a stainless steel or iron saucepan if you can. This type of pan is robust and, unlike most coated pans, will withstand high temperatures. You can replace the pepitas with walnuts or almonds.

The popularity of the dark chocolate and chilli combination goes back to the Aztecs, but the addition of caramelised pepitas is new — and very tasty!

RASPBERRY BROWNIE CAKE

2 tablespoons vegetable oil

2 tablespoons unsweetened cocoa powder

1 egg

¾ cup (140 g) lightly packed soft brown sugar

60 g (2 oz) plain (all-purpose) flour

¼ teaspoon bicarbonate of soda (baking soda)

¼ cup (30 g) coarsely chopped pecans

3 cups (375 g) raspberries

1 tablespoon cornflour (cornstarch) mixed with 2 tablespoons water

--- PREPARATION 15 minutes

--- COOKING 20 minutes

--- SERVES 8

1 Preheat the oven to 180°C (350°F/ Gas 4). Grease a 20 cm (8 inch) cake tin.

2 Combine the oil, cocoa, egg, ¼ cup (60 ml) water, ½ cup (90 g) sugar, all the flour and the bicarbonate of soda in a large bowl. Stir until combined, then fold in the pecans. Pour the mixture into the prepared tin and bake for 20 minutes, or until a skewer inserted in the centre comes out clean. Cool in the tin on a wire rack.

3 Meanwhile, combine half the raspberries and the remaining sugar in a pan and cook, stirring, for 4 minutes, or until the raspberries are juicy. Stir in the cornflour mixture. Cook, stirring, for 4 minutes, or until the mixture is thickened. Strain through a sieve to remove the seeds. Cool for 10 minutes. Spoon over the brownie base and arrange the remaining raspberries on top.

Raspberries and chocolate have a natural affinity that's hard to beat.

APRICOT CHOCOLATE ROLL

SPONGE CAKE

3 eggs

85 g (3 oz) caster (superfine) sugar

45 g (1½ oz) plain (all-purpose) flour

½ teaspoon baking powder

2 tablespoons unsweetened cocoa powder

FILLING AND DECORATION

250 g (8 oz) cream cheese

2–3 tablespoons sugar

1 tablespoon apricot or orange liqueur

½ cup (125 ml) cream, for whipping

4 apricots or 150 g (5 oz) can apricot halves, drained and cut into small pieces

icing (confectioners') sugar, for dusting

⌖ **PREPARATION** 30 minutes

⌖ **COOKING** 12 minutes plus chilling

⌖ **SERVES** 6–8

1 Preheat the oven to 200°C (400°F/Gas 6). Grease a 23 x 33 cm (9 x 13 inch) Swiss roll (jelly roll) tin and line with baking (parchment) paper.

2 To make the sponge cake, beat the eggs and sugar using an electric mixer until light and fluffy. Sift over the flour, baking powder and cocoa and fold in carefully using a metal spoon. Spread the mixture into the prepared tin and bake for 10–12 minutes, or until springy to the touch. Turn out onto another sheet of baking paper and leave to cool for 5 minutes. Peel off the paper. Alternatively, turn out onto a tea towel dusted with icing sugar.

3 Beat the cream cheese, sugar and liqueur using an electric mixer until smooth. Whip the cream until stiff peaks form. Fold in the cream. Spread the cream mixture over the sponge cake, leaving 2.5 cm (1 inch) at the far long edge uncovered.

4 If using fresh apricots, pour boiling water over the apricots; peel and halve them and remove the stones. Cut into small pieces and sprinkle over the cream mixture.

5 Starting from a long side, roll up the sponge cake using the baking paper or tea towel to help. Place the roll on a foil-lined baking tray and refrigerate for 20 minutes. Dust with icing sugar.

MOCHA CREAM ROLL

3 eggs
85 g (3 oz) sugar
1 teaspoon grated orange zest
1 tablespoon orange juice
90 g (3¼ oz) plain (all-purpose)
    flour
½ teaspoon baking powder

FILLING AND DECORATION

100 g (3½ oz) chocolate (mocha
    flavoured, if possible)
1⅔ cups (420 ml) cream, for
    whipping
1 tablespoon cold instant coffee
2 tablespoons icing
    (confectioners') sugar
unsweetened cocoa powder,
    for dusting
chocolate flowers and leaves

·•· PREPARATION 45 minutes
·•· COOKING 10–12 minutes
·•· SERVES 8

You can use dark chocolate
if mocha flavoured isn't available.
Decorate with chocolate-coated
coffee beans or chocolate shavings.

1 Preheat the oven to 200°C (400°F/Gas 6).
Grease a 23 x 33 cm (9 x 13 inch) Swiss roll (jelly
roll) tin and line with baking (parchment) paper.

2 Beat the eggs, sugar, orange zest and juice until
light and fluffy. Sift the flour and baking powder
over the egg mixture; fold in with a whisk.

3 Spread the mixture into the prepared tin and
bake for 10–12 minutes, or until springy to the
touch. Remove from the oven and turn out onto
a sheet of baking paper. Let cool for 5 minutes
then carefully peel off the baking paper and
cover with a tea towel.

4 Melt the chocolate in a bowl over gently
simmering water; cool. Whip the cream until stiff.
Gradually stir in the chocolate, coffee and icing
sugar. Place about ½ cup chocolate cream in a
piping (icing) bag fitted with a large star nozzle.

5 Remove the tin and top sheet of paper from
the cake. Spread three-quarters of the chocolate
cream over the cake. Using the bottom sheet of
baking paper to help keep the roll neat, roll up
the cake, starting from a long side.

6 Spread remaining chocolate cream over cake.
Pipe small rosettes on the top. Dust with cocoa
and decorate with chocolate flowers and leaves.

CHOCOLATE AND COFFEE ROULADE

*W*hipped cream, delicately flavoured with a dash of liqueur, is rolled up in a light and moist roulade. A hint of coffee adds depth of flavour.

1 tablespoon instant coffee granules

1 tablespoon boiling water

100 g (3½ oz) dark chocolate

4 large eggs, separated

125 g (4 oz) caster (superfine) sugar, plus extra for sprinkling

FILLING

300 ml (10 fl oz) cream, for whipping

1 tablespoon brandy or orange liqueur

icing (confectioners') sugar, for dusting

fresh berries or thin orange slices, to decorate

••• PREPARATION 20 minutes

••• COOKING 20 minutes

••• SERVES 8

A roulade can be eaten as is, or dusted with icing sugar and served with fresh fruit for an elegant dessert.

1 Preheat oven to 180°C (350°F/Gas 4). Grease a 28 x 33 cm (11 x 13 inch) Swiss roll (jelly roll) tin and line it with baking (parchment) paper.

2 Dissolve the coffee in the boiling water. Stir until smooth. Break up the chocolate and melt in a heatproof bowl set over a saucepan of barely simmering water, or in the microwave oven, then remove from the heat.

3 Whisk the egg yolks and sugar in a large bowl until thick and pale, then stir in the cold coffee mixture and melted chocolate.

4 Whisk the eggwhites in a separate bowl until stiff. Fold 2 tablespoons of the eggwhites into the chocolate mixture to loosen it, then fold in the remaining eggwhites.

5 Spread the mixture into the prepared tin and bake for about 20 minutes, or until it springs back when lightly pressed with a finger.

6 Remove the tin from the oven and put it on a wire rack. Cover the cake with a clean tea towel (dish towel) and leave it to cool for a few hours or overnight.

7 Sprinkle some caster sugar over a sheet of baking paper, then turn the cake out onto the paper and trim off the crusty edges.

8 Whip the cream lightly, fold in the brandy or liqueur and spread it over the cake. Roll up the cake, using the paper to help you lift it. Dust with icing sugar and decorate with fresh berries or thin slices of orange.

Swiss rolls (jelly rolls) are made from a light sponge cake mixture that contains flour. Roulades are based on a whisked egg mixture and contain very little or no flour. They are moister and softer than Swiss rolls.

To prevent a Swiss roll from cracking when rolled, trim off its crusty edges then, while it is still warm, put it on baking (parchment) paper dusted with caster (superfine) sugar. Roll it up loosely, rolling the paper with it, and leave it to cool in the paper. Then gently open up the roll slightly, remove the paper and spread the interior with jam, lemon or lime curd or cream.

Roulades are easier to roll than Swiss rolls, so can be filled before rolling up, as in the recipe at left. They usually crack when being rolled, but still look attractive when dredged with icing (confectioners') sugar.

TRIPLE-CHOCOLATE ROULADE

*E*veryone will enjoy this warm and light chocolate roll with its rich filling of chocolate spread. It's so quick and easy — ideal for an everyday treat.

3 eggs

150 g (5 oz) caster (superfine) sugar

75 g (2½ oz) plain (all-purpose) flour

45 g (1½ oz) unsweetened cocoa powder

1 tablespoon brandy

½ teaspoon vanilla extract

1 tablespoon butter

1 tablespoon icing (confectioners') sugar

85 g (3 oz) chocolate or chocolate-hazelnut spread

•◦• PREPARATION 10 minutes
•◦• COOKING 10 minutes
•◦• SERVES 6

1 Preheat the oven to 220°C (425°C/ Gas 7). Cover a large baking tray with a sheet of baking (parchment) paper.

2 In a large bowl, beat the eggs and half the caster sugar with an electric mixer on high speed for about 3 minutes, or until pale and very thick; the mixture should hold its shape.

3 Sift the flour and 2 tablespoons cocoa evenly over the mixture, then use a large metal spoon to fold it in.

4 Pour the mixture onto the baking paper and spread it out lightly into a rectangle about 23 x 33 cm (9 x 13 inches). Do not press heavily — it doesn't matter if the edges are not quite square. Bake for 8–10 minutes, or until the sponge cake is risen, set and springy in the middle when lightly pressed.

5 While the sponge cake is baking, put the remaining caster sugar, 2 tablespoons of the remaining cocoa and 150 ml (5 fl oz) water in a saucepan. Bring to a boil, stirring, then boil for 2 minutes. Remove from heat and stir in the brandy, vanilla and butter. Set the syrup aside over a low heat to keep warm.

6 Dampen a clean tea towel (dish towel) with hot water, then lay it on a clean work surface. Lay a sheet of baking paper on top and sift the remaining cocoa and the icing sugar over the paper, covering an area about the size of the cake. Remove the sponge cake from the oven and invert it onto the cocoa and sugar mixture on the paper.

7 Peel off the lining paper and trim off the crisp edges. Make a shallow cut about 1 cm (½ inch) in from a long edge, but don't cut right through the sponge. This will help with rolling it up. Dollop the chocolate spread over the sponge and spread it out thickly — there's no need to be too fussy. Roll up the cake and the filling from the long edge that has the cut, using the cut to start the roll tightly. Hold the paper and the damp cloth to guide the roll, then hold the roll firmly in the cloth for a minute, so that it sets in place.

8 Remove the towel and paper, then sprinkle the cocoa mixture over the sponge. Don't worry if the roll is slightly cracked. Cut six slices of roll, using a serrated knife, arrange on serving plates, then spoon the hot syrup over the top.

For an alcohol-free version, omit the brandy.

For an easy yet decadent home-baked dessert in next to no time, just add a scoop of vanilla ice-cream for the perfect balance.

CHOCOLATE LOG

3 eggs
1 cup (230 g) caster (superfine) sugar
1 teaspoon vanilla extract
75 g (2½ oz) plain (all-purpose) flour
1 teaspoon baking powder
¼ teaspoon salt
¼ cup (30 g) icing (confectioners')
    sugar, plus extra for dusting
3 cups (540 g) vanilla ice-cream,
    softened
350 g (12 oz) dark chocolate

• PREPARATION 15 minutes
• COOKING 15 minutes plus freezing
• SERVES 10

1 Preheat the oven to 180°C (350°F/Gas 4). Grease a 28 x 33 cm (11 x 13 inch) Swiss roll (jelly roll) tin and line it with baking (parchment) paper. Grease the paper.

2 Beat the eggs with an electric mixer for 3 minutes. Gradually add the caster sugar, beating for 2 minutes, or until the mixture is thick and pale. Stir in ⅓ cup (80 ml) water and the vanilla. Sift the flour, baking powder and salt over the egg mixture and beat until smooth.

3 Spread the mixture evenly into the prepared tin. Bake for 12–15 minutes, or until the cake springs back when lightly touched. Cool for 5 minutes.

4 Invert the cake onto a tea towel (dish towel) dusted with icing sugar. Gently peel off the lining paper. Roll up the cake, enclosing the towel, starting with a short side. Cool completely on a wire rack.

5 Unroll the cake; spread evenly with ice-cream to within 1 cm (½ inch) of edges. Roll up again, without the towel. Place, seam side down, on a serving plate. Cover and freeze for at least 1 hour.

6 Melt 125 g (4 oz) of the chocolate and spread over a baking tray lined with baking paper. Refrigerate for 30 minutes. Break the chilled chocolate into pieces about 3 x 8 cm (1 x 3 inches). Melt the remaining chocolate and spread it over the top, side and ends of the cake. Working quickly, place the chocolate pieces on the cake to resemble bark. Freeze. Remove from the freezer 10 minutes before cutting. Dust with icing sugar to serve.

SLICES, BROWNIES AND MUFFINS

CHOCOLATE CHERRY SLICE

250 g (8 oz) plain digestive
    biscuits (graham crackers)
150 g (5 oz) butter, melted

FILLING

400 g (14 oz) can sweetened
    condensed milk
2¾ cups (250 g) desiccated
    coconut
1⅔ cups (400 g) finely chopped
    glacé (candied) cherries
100 g (3½ oz) white vegetable
    shortening, such as Copha,
    Kremalta, Trex or Crisco,
    melted

TOPPING

200 g (7 oz) dark chocolate,
    roughly chopped
1 tablespoon white vegetable
    shortening, such as Copha,
    Kremalta, Trex or Crisco

- PREPARATION 20 minutes plus setting
- COOKING Nil
- MAKES 24

1 Line a 20 x 30 cm (8 x 12 inch) baking tin with baking (parchment) paper.

2 Process the biscuits in a food processor until finely chopped. Combine the crumbs and melted butter and press evenly into the prepared tin. Chill in the freezer while preparing the topping.

3 Combine all the filling ingredients in a large bowl and mix well. Press the filling evenly over the base, using wet hands to smooth the surface.

4 To make the topping, melt the chocolate and shortening in a heatproof bowl over a saucepan of simmering water, ensuring the base of the bowl does not touch the water. Stir until melted, then spread evenly over the cherry filling.

5 Leave to harden at room temperature for up to 1 hour (depending on the weather). Cut into 5 cm (2 inch) squares using a hot knife. Store in an airtight container for up to 3 days.

Solid vegetable shortenings include Crisco, made from vegetable oil, and Copha, made from coconut oil. Unlike other oils and fats, they stay solid at room temperature. They are white at room temperature but turn clear when melted.

WHITE CHOCOLATE CRANBERRY MUESLI SLICE

¼ cup (55 g) sugar

¼ cup (90 g) honey

¼ cup (60 ml) maple syrup

2 tablespoons reduced-fat peanut butter

1 eggwhite

1 tablespoon low-fat evaporated milk

1 teaspoon vanilla extract

150 g (5 oz) wholemeal plain (all-purpose) flour

½ teaspoon bicarbonate of soda (baking soda)

½ teaspoon ground cinnamon

¼ teaspoon ground allspice

2 cups (200 g) original (rolled) porridge oats

1½ cups (45 g) puffed rice cereal

⅓ cup (50 g) white chocolate chips

¼ cup (30 g) sweetened dried cranberries

¼ cup (30 g) chopped walnuts

⁌ PREPARATION 10 minutes

⁌ COOKING 20 minutes

⁌ MAKES 24

1 Preheat the oven to 180°C (350°F/Gas 4). Grease a 23 x 33 cm (9 x 13 inch) baking tin.

2 In a large bowl, combine the sugar, honey, maple syrup, peanut butter, eggwhite, evaporated milk and vanilla. Sift the flour, bicarbonate of soda, cinnamon and allspice over the sugar mixture and stir in, also adding any bran from the sieve. Stir in the oats, cereal, chocolate chips, cranberries and walnuts.

3 Press into the prepared tin and bake for 18–20 minutes, or until golden brown. Cool in the tin on a wire rack. Cut into bars. Store, covered, in the refrigerator.

Full of nutritious oats, nuts, dried fruit and spices, these make a healthy and economical alternative to bought muesli bars.

CHOCOLATE PEPPERMINT SLICE

250 g (8 oz) plain chocolate-
    flavoured biscuits (cookies)
150 g (5 oz) butter, melted
2 cups (250 g) pure icing
    (confectioners') sugar, sifted
1 teaspoon peppermint extract
2–3 tablespoons milk
200 g (7 oz) dark chocolate,
    roughly chopped
1 tablespoon vegetable oil

PREPARATION 20 minutes
    plus 10 minutes setting
COOKING Nil
MAKES 24

A lovely treat for after dinner — or any time, really. The finer the grade of chocolate you use, the better the flavour will be.

1 Grease a 20 x 30 cm (8 x 12 inch) baking tin and line the base and sides with baking (parchment) paper.

2 Process the biscuits in a food processor until finely chopped. Combine the crumbs and melted butter and press evenly into the prepared tin. Place the tin in the freezer while you prepare the topping.

3 In a bowl, mix together the icing sugar, peppermint and 2 tablespoons milk — the mixture should be a spreading consistency, so add a little more milk if necessary. Spread the icing over the hardened biscuit base and return to the freezer.

4 Melt the chocolate in a heatproof bowl set over a saucepan of barely simmering water, ensuring the base of the bowl does not touch the water. Stir until melted, then stir in the oil.

5 Spread the chocolate over the peppermint layer. Leave for about 10 minutes, or until set. To serve, cut into 5 cm (2 inch) squares using a hot knife. Store in an airtight container in the refrigerator for up to 3 days.

ALMOND COCONUT BARS

1½ cups (185 g) digestive biscuit
(graham cracker) crumbs
125 g (4 oz) butter, melted
400 g (14 oz) can sweetened
condensed milk
200 g (7 oz) flaked coconut
2 cups (350 g) dark chocolate chips
½ cup (125 g) smooth peanut
butter
24 almonds

•→ PREPARATION 15 minutes
•→ COOKING 20 minutes plus chilling
•→ MAKES 24

1 Preheat oven to 180°C (350°F/Gas 4).

2 In a small bowl, combine the crumbs
and butter. Press into an ungreased 23 x
33 cm (9 x 13 inch) baking tin. Combine
the condensed milk and coconut, and
carefully spread over the crust. Bake for
18–20 minutes, or until lightly browned.

3 Melt the chocolate chips and peanut
butter in a heatproof bowl set over a
saucepan of barely simmering water,
or in the microwave. Stir until smooth.

4 Spread over the warm crust and garnish
with almonds. Refrigerate in the tin for
1 hour before cutting into bars.

CHOCOLATE PEANUT SQUARES

250 g (8 oz) butter

175 g (6 oz) dark chocolate, chopped

1½ cups (185 g) digestive biscuit (graham cracker) crumbs

½ cup (80 g) unsalted dry-roasted peanuts, chopped

500 g (1 lb) cream cheese, softened

1 cup (220 g) sugar

1 teaspoon vanilla extract

•◦ PREPARATION 15 minutes plus chilling

•◦ COOKING Nil

•◦ MAKES 24

1 Grease a 23 cm x 33 cm (9 x 13 inch) baking tin.

2 Melt 185 g (6 oz) butter and 60 g (2 oz) chocolate in a heatproof bowl set over simmering water. Stir until smooth. Stir in crumbs and nuts. Cover and refrigerate for 30 minutes, or until set.

3 In a small bowl, beat the cream cheese, sugar and vanilla until fluffy. Spread over the chocolate layer. Melt the remaining butter and chocolate. Stir until smooth, then carefully spread over the cream cheese layer. Cover and refrigerate until set. Cut into squares and store in the refrigerator.

CLASSIC BROWNIES

250 g (8 oz) unsalted butter, chopped

200 g (7 oz) dark chocolate, chopped, plus ⅔ cup (100 g) dark chocolate chunks or dark chocolate chips

1¾ cups (325 g) lightly packed soft brown sugar

4 eggs, lightly beaten

1 teaspoon vanilla extract

185 g (6 oz) plain (all-purpose) flour, sifted

icing (confectioners') sugar, for dusting (optional)

•• PREPARATION 20 minutes

•• COOKING 40 minutes

•• MAKES 12

For triple-choc brownies, replace dark chocolate chunks or chips with ⅓ cup (50 g) white chocolate chips and ⅓ cup (50 g) milk chocolate chips. For walnut or macadamia brownies, add 1¼ cups (150 g) chopped walnuts or macadamias with the chocolate chips.

1 Preheat the oven to 170°C (340°F/ Gas 3). Grease an 18 x 28 cm (7 x 11 inch) baking tin and line the base and sides with baking (parchment) paper.

2 Melt the butter and the 200 g (7 oz) chopped chocolate in a saucepan over low heat. Whisk in sugar until combined, then leave for 5 minutes to cool.

3 Whisk in the eggs and vanilla, then stir in the flour. Add the chocolate chunks or chips and stir to combine.

4 Pour the mixture into the prepared tin and bake for 35 minutes, or until the top is firm and looks dry and the cake is coming away from the sides of the tin — it should still be very moist inside.

5 Remove from the oven and allow to cool completely in the tin. Cut into pieces and store in an airtight container at room temperature for up to 4 days. Serve dusted with icing sugar if desired.

FUDGY BROWNIES

85 g (3 oz) dark chocolate
(at least 70 per cent cocoa)
100 g (3½ oz) unsalted butter
½ cup (115 g) caster (superfine)
sugar
½ cup (95 g) lightly packed soft
brown sugar
1 teaspoon vanilla extract
2 whole eggs and 1 egg yolk,
at room temperature, beaten
together
100 g (3½ oz) plain (all-purpose)
flour
¼ cup (30 g) unsweetened cocoa
powder

- PREPARATION 15 minutes
- COOKING About 30 minutes
- MAKES 16

1 Preheat the oven to 180°C (350°F/
Gas 4). Grease an 18 cm (7 inch) square
shallow cake tin and line the base with
baking (parchment) paper.

2 Break up the chocolate, chop the
butter, and melt both in a heatproof bowl
set over a saucepan of simmering water,
making sure the base of the bowl does
not touch the water. Leave until melted,
then remove the bowl from the heat and
allow to cool.

3 Stir the sugars and vanilla into the
chocolate mixture. Gradually beat in the
egg mixture. Sift the flour and cocoa over
the chocolate mixture, and stir until
evenly blended. Do not overmix.

Most people's ideal brownie is one that is moist in the centre, almost gooey, and with a rich, deep chocolate flavour.

4 Pour the mixture into the prepared tin and bake for about 30 minutes, or until risen but still slightly soft in the middle; a skewer inserted in the centre should come out with a few moist crumbs still sticking to it. The surface should look dry and cracked.

5 Cool in the tin on a wire rack for 5 minutes, then turn out onto the rack to cool completely. When cold, peel off the lining paper and cut into 16 squares. If possible, wrap the brownies in foil and leave them until the next day before eating. They can be kept like this for 3–4 days.

This recipe uses both chocolate and cocoa powder, which gives the brownies plenty of chocolate flavour. Brown sugar helps produce the desired fudgy texture.

For a nutty version, fold in 60 g (2 oz) coarsely chopped pecans after adding the flour mixture.

It is important not to overcook brownies, or they will be dry. Undercook the mixture in preference to overcooking it — it will continue to cook a little more in the residual heat, and will also firm up on cooling.

CHOCOLATE SQUARES

*C*raving some chocolate? Each one of these luscious little gems is a low-fat, low-cholesterol treat. So go ahead and indulge yourself!

→ **PREPARATION** 15 minutes
→ **COOKING** 45 minutes
→ **MAKES** 36

200 g (7 oz) self-raising flour
85 g (3 oz) unsweetened cocoa
    powder, plus 2 teaspoons extra
⅓ cup (80 ml) buttermilk
1 tablespoon instant espresso
    powder
1 cup (230 g) caster (superfine)
    sugar
½ cup (115 g) firmly packed soft
    brown sugar
250 g (8 oz) apple sauce
2 teaspoons vanilla extract
2 large eggwhites
½ cup (90 g) chocolate chips or
    coarsely grated dark chocolate
1 tablespoon icing (confectioners')
    sugar

1 Preheat the oven to 160°C (320°F/ Gas 2–3). Line a 20 cm (8 inch) square cake tin with foil, letting it overhang about 10 cm (4 inches) on two opposite sides.

2 Sift the flour and 85 g (3 oz) cocoa powder into a large bowl. Heat the buttermilk and espresso powder in a small saucepan over a low heat and stir until the coffee has dissolved.

3 Mix the caster and brown sugars, apple sauce and vanilla in a bowl. Pour in the hot buttermilk mixture, then add the flour mixture and stir until just blended.

4 Whisk the eggwhites until soft peaks form. Fold the eggwhites and chocolate chips into the flour mixture.

5 Spoon into the prepared tin and bake for about 45 minutes, or until just set (do not overbake). Cool in the tin on a wire rack for 15 minutes, then lift out onto the rack to cool completely. Sift the icing sugar and remaining cocoa over the cake. Cut into 4 cm (1½ inch) squares to serve.

 This recipe uses apple sauce instead of oil. The slight apple flavour that the sauce imparts complements the coffee–chocolate combination.

 Add 1 tablespoon coffee liqueur to the mixture for an adults-only version.

Sift the flour and cocoa into a large bowl. If you don't have a sifter, use a sieve.

Fold the eggwhites gently into the cake batter using a rubber spatula.

Lift the cake from the tin by grasping the foil collar; and allow to cool completely.

CHOCOLATE WALNUT BROWNIES

*F*ew people can resist chocolate. Put it in a brownie and it gets even better. Try serving this version as a quick and easy dessert with ice-cream and chocolate sauce.

125 g (4 oz) butter, softened
200 g (7 oz) dark chocolate, chopped
2 eggs
1 cup (230 g) caster (superfine) sugar
1 teaspoon vanilla extract
60 g (2 oz) plain (all-purpose) flour
2 tablespoons unsweetened cocoa powder
1 cup (100 g) roughly chopped walnuts

PREPARATION 25 minutes
COOKING 30 minutes
MAKES 20–24

1 Preheat the oven to 180°C (350°F/Gas 4). Grease a 20 cm (8 inch) square cake tin and line the base and sides with baking (parchment) paper.

2 Melt the butter and 125 g (4 oz) chocolate in a heatproof bowl set over a saucepan of simmering water. Remove from the heat and leave to cool.

3 Beat the eggs using an electric mixer. Gradually add the sugar, beating continuously until the mixture is thick and foamy and leaves a ribbon-like trail when the beaters are lifted. Add the vanilla and the chocolate mixture and blend in thoroughly. Sift the flour and cocoa over the mixture. Add the walnuts and the remaining chocolate. Fold together with a large spoon.

4 Pour into the prepared tin and bake for about 30 minutes, or until the top is a rich brown. (Place a piece of foil over the top if it looks to be in danger of burning.) Cool briefly in the tin, then cut into squares and lift out onto a wire rack to cool completely. Store in an airtight container; they will keep for 3–4 days.

BLONDIES

Grease a 20 x 30 cm (8 x 12 inch) baking tin. In a large bowl using an electric mixer, beat 2 cups (360 g) lightly packed brown sugar and 160 g (5½ oz) butter until light and fluffy. Using a wooden spoon, stir in 2 eggs, one at a time, and ½ teaspoon almond or vanilla extract. Sift 190 g (6½ oz) plain (all-purpose) flour, 1 teaspoon baking powder and ½ teaspoon bicarbonate of soda (baking soda) over the butter mixture. Stir in. Chop 175 g (6 oz) white chocolate; stir half into the mixture. Spoon the mixture into the prepared tin and sprinkle the top with the rest of the white chocolate. Bake for 35–40 minutes. Cool in the tin, then cut into 18 squares.

◈ The hallmarks of a good brownie are a dense chocolate flavour and a fudge-like texture. The texture is achieved by the high proportion of sugar and butter to flour, and by not over-cooking the mixture. It's also important to use a good-quality chocolate.

◈ For a chocolate topping, beat 125 g (4 oz) butter with ¾ cup (90 g) icing (confectioners') sugar until creamy. Beat in 1 tablespoon water alternately with a further ¼ cup (30 g) icing sugar. Beat in a few drops of vanilla extract and 30 g (1 oz) melted dark or white chocolate.

◈ Add a dash of brandy or almond liqueur to the cake batter.

RASPBERRY TRUFFLE BROWNIES

1¼ cups (185 g) chopped dark
    chocolate

125 g (4 oz) butter, cubed

2 eggs

1 cup (220 g) sugar

1 teaspoon vanilla extract

150 g (5 oz) plain (all-purpose)
    flour

¼ teaspoon bicarbonate of soda
    (baking soda)

¼ teaspoon salt

1 cup (125 g) fresh raspberries

ICING

1¼ cups (185 g) chopped dark
    chocolate

175 ml (6 fl oz) thickened (heavy/
    double) whipping cream

2 tablespoons seedless raspberry
    jam

1 teaspoon vanilla extract

12 fresh raspberries

mint leaves, to garnish

⋅⋅➤ PREPARATION 20 minutes

⋅⋅➤ COOKING 30 minutes

⋅⋅➤ MAKES 12

1 Grease a 23 cm (9 inch) square shallow cake tin. Preheat the oven to 180°C (350°F/Gas 4).

2 Melt chocolate and butter in a heatproof bowl set over a saucepan of simmering water, or in the microwave; stir until smooth. In a bowl, beat the eggs, sugar and vanilla. Stir in the chocolate mixture. Combine flour, bicarbonate of soda and salt; gradually add to the chocolate mixture, then fold in the raspberries. Spoon into the tin, level the top and bake for 25–30 minutes, or until a skewer inserted in the centre comes out clean (do not overbake). Cool in the tin on a wire rack.

3 For the icing (frosting), in a small microwave-safe bowl, microwave the chocolate, cream and jam at 50 per cent power for 2–3 minutes, or until smooth, stirring twice. Stir in the vanilla. Place the bowl in a bowl of iced water, stir for 3–5 minutes, then beat on medium speed until soft peaks form.

4 Fill a piping (icing) bag fitted with a star tip with ½ cup (60 g) of the icing. Spread the remaining icing over the top of the brownies. Cut into 12 bars. Pipe a chocolate rosette in the centre of each brownie; top with a raspberry and mint leaves. Cover and refrigerate for 30 minutes, or until the icing is set. Store in the refrigerator.

CHOCOLATE PECAN BROWNIES

125 g (4 oz) butter

125 g (4 oz) dark chocolate

2 eggs

1 cup (230 g) caster (superfine) sugar

1 teaspoon vanilla extract

75 g (2½ oz) plain (all-purpose) flour

1 cup (100 g) pecans or walnuts, roughly chopped

⁎ PREPARATION 25 minutes

⁎ COOKING 30 minutes

⁎ MAKES 20–24

1 Preheat the oven to 180°C (350°F/Gas 4). Grease a 20 cm (8 inch) square cake tin and line it with baking (parchment) paper.

2 Melt the butter and chocolate in a small saucepan over very low heat. Remove from heat and let cool. Beat the eggs in a bowl with an electric mixer. Gradually add the sugar, beating continuously.

3 Continue beating until the mixture is thick and foamy and leaves a ribbon-like trail when the beaters are lifted. Blend in the vanilla and chocolate mixture. Sift the flour over the top, add the walnuts, then fold together with a large spoon. Spoon into the prepared tin and bake for about 30 minutes, or until the top is a rich brown.

4 Cool slightly in the tin on a wire rack, then cut into squares and lift out onto the rack to cool completely. Store in an airtight container for 3–4 days.

꙳ To ice the brownies, beat 125 g (4 oz) butter with ¾ cup (90 g) icing (confectioner's) sugar until creamy. Beat in 1 tablespoon water alternately with a further ¾ cup (90 g) icing sugar. Lastly, beat in a few drops of vanilla extract and 30 g melted dark or white chocolate.

These are chewy and fudgy, and ideal with a cup of coffee. For a brilliant dessert, serve with whipped cream and strawberries.

CHOCOLATE BRANDY SQUARES

⅔ cup (110 g) pitted prunes
100 ml (3½ fl oz) brandy or port
125 g (4 oz) butter, diced
150 g (5 oz) dark chocolate (70 per
    cent cocoa), roughly chopped
2 cups (460 g) caster (superfine)
    sugar
450 g (1 lb) plain (all-purpose) flour
75 g (2½ oz) self-raising flour
85 g (3 oz) unsweetened cocoa
    powder
1 whole egg plus 2 eggwhites, lightly
    beaten together
icing (confectioners') sugar or cocoa
    powder, to serve

⤙ PREPARATION 30 minutes plus standing
⤙ COOKING 1 hour 20 minutes
⤙ MAKES 16 squares

1 Put a kettle of water on to boil. Heat the oven to 160°C (320°F/Gas 2–3). Grease a 23 cm (9 inch) square cake tin and line with baking (parchment) paper.

2 Purée the prunes in a food processor or electric mixer, adding 1 tablespoon hot water if needed to get a smooth purée. Scrape the purée into a large bowl.

Add the brandy, butter, chocolate, sugar and 1 cup (250 ml) boiling water.

3 Pour the rest of the boiling water into a saucepan, bring to a simmer over low heat and place the bowl on top. Ensure the bottom does not touch the water.

4 Stir frequently until the chocolate melts and the mixture is smooth. Take the bowl off the pan and leave the mixture to cool for 2–3 minutes, or until lukewarm.

5 Sift the flours and cocoa into a separate large bowl and make a well in the centre. Pour in the chocolate mixture, then add the egg mixture and beat until smooth.

6 Pour into the prepared tin and smooth the surface. Bake for 1 hour 15 minutes, or until a skewer inserted in the centre of the cake comes out clean.

7 Cool in the tin on a wire rack for 15 minutes, then turn out onto the wire rack to cool completely. Dust the cake with sifted icing sugar or cocoa and cut into 16 squares. This cake will keep well if wrapped in foil.

CHOCOLATE MUFFINS WITH CHOCOLATE FILLING

200 g (7 oz) plain (all-purpose) flour
50 g (1¾ oz) unsweetened cocoa
    powder
1½ teaspoons baking powder
pinch salt
100 g (3½ oz) butter, softened
150 g (5 oz) sugar
1 teaspoon vanilla extract
2 eggs
buttermilk or milk, if needed

CHOCOLATE FILLING

100 g (3½ oz) dark chocolate
150 g (5 oz) butter, softened
150 g (5 oz) icing (confectioners')
    sugar
1½ teaspoons vanilla extract

⸱⸱► PREPARATION 30 minutes
⸱⸱► COOKING 20 minutes
⸱⸱► MAKES 12

*For those who think that too much chocolate
is never enough, this recipe should
be very much to your taste!*

1 Preheat the oven to 180°C (350°F)/Gas 4). Line a 12-hole standard (1/3 cup/80 ml) muffin tin with paper cases, or use silicone moulds.

2 In a bowl, sift together the flour, cocoa, baking powder and salt. In a separate bowl, beat the butter, sugar and vanilla until light and creamy. Beat in the eggs, one at a time, then fold in the flour mixture. If the mixture is too firm, mix in a little buttermilk or milk.

3 Fill the paper cases two-thirds full with the mixture and bake for about 20 minutes, or until the tops have risen and the muffins are springy to the touch. Cool in the tin on a wire rack for 10 minutes, then lift out onto the rack to cool completely.

4 To make the filling, chop the chocolate and melt in a heatproof bowl set over a saucepan of simmering water. Remove from the heat and allow to cool to room temperature.

5 Beat the butter, icing sugar and vanilla with an electric mixer until fluffy. Add the melted chocolate and beat until smooth, starting with the mixer on low speed then increasing to medium.

6 Cut the top off each muffin to form a lid. Reserve a small amount of the filling, and pipe or spread the remainder onto the bottom half of each muffin. Place the lids over the chocolate topping on each muffin. On each lid, pipe or dollop some chocolate filling mixture. Garnish with silver cachous if desired.

CHOCOLATE MUFFINS

100 g (3½ oz) dark chocolate
(at least 60 per cent cocoa),
chopped
125 g (4 oz) butter, chopped
150 g (5 oz) caster (superfine)
sugar
2 eggs, lightly beaten
175 g (6 oz) sour cream
¼ cup (60 ml) brandy
¼ teaspoon ground cinnamon
pinch ground cardamom
210 g (7½ oz) plain (all-purpose)
flour
1 teaspoon baking powder
3 tablespoons unsweetened cocoa
powder

•→ PREPARATION 25 minutes
•→ COOKING 25 minutes
•→ MAKES 12

1 Preheat the oven to 180°C (350°F/Gas 4). Line a 12-hole standard (⅓ cup/80 ml) muffin tin with paper cases, or use silicone moulds.

2 Melt the chocolate and butter in a heatproof bowl set over a saucepan of simmering water. Cool. Stir in the sugar, eggs, sour cream, brandy and spices.

3 Sift the flour, baking powder and cocoa into a bowl. Stir in the chocolate mixture.

4 Fill the paper cases two-thirds full and bake for 20–25 minutes. Cool in the tin on a wire rack for a few minutes before serving, or allow to cool completely then serve.

To make sure that muffins are featherlight, do not mix the batter too vigorously. For best results, mix the liquid and dry ingredients with a wooden spoon, not an electric mixer. Mix briefly so the ingredients are only just blended.

For Chocolate Muffins with Cherries, use 4 tablespoons Kirsch instead of brandy. Before baking, gently fold 200 g (7 oz) pitted cherries into the batter. Sprinkle flaked almonds on top.

For an extra treat, ice the cooled muffins and decorate them with chocolate sprinkles.

Chocolate-Chip and Banana Muffins

1½ tablespoons vegetable oil

200 g (7 oz) peeled bananas, coarsely chopped

1 whole egg plus 2 eggwhites

1 cup (250 ml) low-fat milk

450 g (1 lb) self-raising flour

150 g (5 oz) caster (superfine) sugar or soft brown sugar

½ teaspoon bicarbonate of soda (baking soda)

2 teaspoons finely grated orange zest

60 g (2 oz) dark chocolate (70 per cent cocoa), finely chopped

•→ PREPARATION 15 minutes

•→ COOKING 25 minutes

•→ MAKES 12

1 Preheat the oven to 190°C (375°F/Gas 5). Using a pastry brush and half the oil, lightly grease a 12-hole standard (⅓ cup/80 ml) muffin tin, or line it with paper cases or silicone moulds.

2 Using a food processor or electric mixer, purée the bananas with the remaining oil, the whole egg, eggwhites and milk.

3 Sift the flour, sugar and bicarbonate of soda into a large mixing bowl. Stir in the orange zest and chocolate. Fold in the banana mixture until just blended; do not overmix. It does not matter if a little flour remains unincorporated.

4 Spoon the mixture into the prepared muffin tin, filling the cups about two-thirds full. Bake for 25 minutes, or until the muffins have risen and are lightly browned.

5 Remove from the oven and take the muffins out of the tin. Serve hot or at room temperature, preferably on the day of baking.

Chocolate can be part of a healthy diet, as these delicious muffins prove. They use the best-quality chocolate to give more flavour with less fat.

CHOCOLATE APPLE MUFFINS

175 g (6 oz) marzipan paste, at
    room temperature, chopped
2 eggs, lightly beaten
85 g (3 oz) butter, softened
200 ml (7 fl oz) buttermilk
85 g (3 oz) caster (superfine) sugar
2 tablespoons hazelnut spread
1/2 teaspoon ground cinnamon
1/2 tablespoon unsweetened cocoa
    powder
210 g (7 1/2 oz) plain (all-purpose)
    flour
1 teaspoon baking powder
2 tart apples
flaked almonds, for decoration

⤙ **PREPARATION** 30 minutes
⤙ **COOKING** 20 minutes
⤙ **MAKES** 24

1 Preheat the oven to 180°C (350°F/Gas 4).
Grease two 12-hole standard (1/3 cup/80 ml)
muffin tins, or line them with paper cases or
silicone moulds.

2 Beat the marzipan, eggs and butter with a
wooden spoon until smooth. Gradually mix in
the buttermilk, sugar and hazelnut spread with
a wooden spoon until light and fluffy.

3 Sift the cinnamon, cocoa, flour and baking
powder into a large bowl. Add the marzipan
mixture and stir until just combined.

4 Peel, halve and core the apples. Cut into
small cubes and stir into the flour and marzipan
mixture. Spoon into the tins or cases, filling them
two-thirds full. Sprinkle with flaked almonds.
Bake for about 20 minutes, or until golden
brown. Cool in the tins on a wire rack.

ᔧ When greasing tins for muffins and
cupcakes, or trays for cookies, use a light hand
unless the recipe says otherwise. You just want
enough covering to prevent the mixture from
sticking. Too thick a coating may cause muffins
to be gluey, and cookies to spread too much.

BISCUITS AND COOKIES

CHOC-CHIP BISCUITS

125 g (4 oz) butter
⅓ cup (80 g) caster (superfine)
   sugar
1 teaspoon vanilla extract
2 tablespoons sweetened
   condensed milk
150 g (5 oz) self-raising flour
125 g (4 oz) dark chocolate, finely
   chopped
sifted icing (confectioners') sugar,
   for dusting

⊷ **PREPARATION** 15 minutes
⊷ **COOKING** 15 minutes per tray
⊷ **MAKES** 30

1 Preheat the oven to 160°C (320°F/Gas 2–3). Grease 2 baking trays or line them with baking (parchment) paper.

2 Using an electric mixer, beat the butter, sugar and vanilla until light and creamy. Add the condensed milk and beat well. Fold in the flour and chocolate.

3 Drop half-tablespoons of the mixture about 5 cm (2 inches) apart onto the prepared trays. Bake for 15 minutes. Cool on the trays for 3 minutes, then carefully transfer to wire racks to cool completely.

4 Lightly dust with icing sugar and store in an airtight container lined with paper towels for up to 4 days.

🐦 For a chunkier texture, replace the chopped chocolate with 125 (4 oz) chocolate chips. Use dark, milk or white chocolate, as you prefer, or a mixture.

Choc-chip biscuits must be one of the most universally popular biscuits of all time.

CHOCOLATE OATMEAL CRUNCH

125 g (4 oz) plain (all-purpose)
    flour
½ teaspoon bicarbonate of soda
    (baking soda)
½ teaspoon salt
1 cup (100 g) original rolled
    (porridge) oats
60 g (2 oz) butter
125 g (4 oz) soft brown sugar
½ cup (110 g) sugar
1 large egg
1 teaspoon vanilla extract
⅓ cup (90 g) low-fat sour cream
¾ cup (130 g) dark chocolate
    chips

•·· PREPARATION 15 minutes
•·· COOKING 10 minutes per tray
•·· MAKES 36

1 Preheat the oven to 190°C (375°F/Gas 5). Grease 2 large baking trays or line them with baking (parchment) paper. Sift the flour, bicarbonate of soda and salt into a bowl. Stir in the oats.

2 Beat the butter and sugars in a large bowl using an electric mixer on high speed until light and creamy. Add the egg and vanilla and beat for a further 3 minutes, until the mixture is pale yellow and light. Add the sour cream and use a wooden spoon to combine. Add the flour mixture all at once and mix until just combined. Don't overmix or the cookies may become tough. Stir in the chocolate chips.

3 Drop teaspoonfuls of the dough about 5 cm (2 inches) apart onto the prepared trays. Bake for about 10 minutes, or until golden. Cool on the trays for 2 minutes, then transfer to wire racks to cool completely. Store in an airtight container for up to 2 weeks or freeze for up to 3 months.

⌇ The low-fat sour cream helps keep the melt-in-your-mouth quality high and the fat content low. The rolled (porridge) oats add an extra helping of heart-healthy goodness.

LOW-FAT CHOCOLATE-CHIP BISCUITS

*F*lecks of grated chocolate replace the traditional chocolate chips in this healthier version of a favourite American cookie.

150 g (5 oz) plain (all-purpose) flour, sifted

45 g (1½ oz) wholemeal (whole-wheat) plain (all-purpose) flour, unsifted

½ teaspoon bicarbonate of soda (baking soda)

60 g (2 oz) unsalted butter

60 g (2 oz) sugar

60 g (2 oz) soft brown sugar

1 large egg

1 large eggwhite

2 teaspoons vanilla extract

30 g (1 oz) dark chocolate, finely grated

·•· PREPARATION 10 minutes

·•· COOKING About 10 minutes per tray

·•· MAKES About 36

1 Preheat the oven to 190°C (375°F/Gas 5). In a small bowl, combine the flours and bicarbonate of soda and set aside.

2 In a large bowl using an electric mixer, beat the butter and sugars at moderately low speed for 2 minutes, or until light and creamy. Beat in the egg, eggwhite and vanilla.

3 Using a wooden spoon, mix in the dry ingredients and the chocolate.

4 Drop rounded teaspoonfuls of the dough about 5 cm (2 inches) apart onto ungreased baking trays. Bake for 8–10 minutes, or until lightly browned around the edges. Transfer immediately to wire racks to cool.

CHOCOLATE–NUT MERINGUE BISCUITS

*H*ere's an astounding achievement: chocolate–nut biscuits with less than one gram of fat each! The secret is the meringue base.

1/3 cup (40 g) walnuts
1/2 cup (60 g) icing (confectioners') sugar, plus 2 tablespoons extra for dusting
1 tablespoon unsweetened cocoa powder
1/4 teaspoon ground cinnamon
2 large eggwhites

- **PREPARATION** 10 minutes
- **COOKING** 20 minutes per tray
- **MAKES** 36

Meringues are sensitive to humidity (they'll absorb moisture and become sticky), so bake them on a fairly dry day. Put them in an airtight container once they've cooled completely. If you live in a humid climate, seal the meringues in a freezer bag and freeze them.

1 Preheat the oven to 150°C (300°F/Gas 2). Line 2 baking trays with baking (parchment) paper. Toast the walnuts in a small saucepan, stirring frequently, for about 7 minutes, or until fragrant. When cool enough to handle, chop coarsely.

2 Sift together the icing sugar, cocoa and cinnamon.

3 In a large bowl using an electric mixer, beat the eggwhites until stiff peaks form. Gently fold in the cocoa mixture with a spatula, then gently fold in the walnuts.

4 Drop generous teaspoonfuls of the mixture 2 cm (1 inch) apart onto the prepared trays. Bake for about 20 minutes, or until set. Cool on the trays for a few minutes, then transfer to wire racks to cool completely. Dust with icing sugar just before serving.

These dainty little biscuits contain no butter or margarine and no egg yolks, yet they're tender and rich tasting.

CHOCOLATE MERINGUE DROPS

*S*o tempting, these treats are just the thing if you're craving something sweet yet don't want to overindulge.

2 large eggwhites
½ cup (110 g) sugar
1 teaspoon vanilla extract
2 tablespoons unsweetened cocoa powder
½ cup (85 g) dark chocolate chips

•➤• PREPARATION 8 minutes
•➤• COOKING 1 hour plus drying
•➤• MAKES About 40

Do not make baked meringues or meringue desserts in rainy or humid weather. The meringue will be soggy, not crisp.

1 Preheat the oven to 120°C (250°F/Gas ¼–½). Line 2 baking trays with baking (parchment) paper or foil.

2 In a large bowl using an electric mixer, beat the eggwhites at moderately high speed until stiff peaks form. Beat in the sugar, 1 tablespoon at a time, then beat in the vanilla. Reduce the speed to low and beat in the cocoa. With a spatula, fold in the chocolate chips.

3 Drop rounded teaspoonfuls of the mixture 2.5 cm (1 inch) apart onto the prepared trays. Bake for 1 hour. Turn off the oven and leave the meringues in the oven to dry for a further 2 hours. Store in an airtight container.

CHOCOLATE NUT MERINGUE DROPS

Substitute ½ cup (60 g) coarsely chopped walnuts, pecans or almonds for the chocolate chips, adding a pinch each of ground cinnamon and ground nutmeg to the beaten eggwhites.

BIG CHOCOLATE AND NUT COOKIES

85 g (3 oz) butter

250 g (8 oz) dark chocolate, chopped

2 eggs

¾ cup (170 g) caster (superfine) sugar

2 teaspoons instant coffee granules

1 tablespoon boiling water

2 teaspoons vanilla extract

30 g (1 oz) plain (all-purpose) flour

½ teaspoon salt

¼ teaspoon baking powder

175 g (6 oz) dark chocolate chips

1 cup (125 g) coarsely chopped walnuts

1 cup (120 g) coarsely chopped pecans

⌁ PREPARATION 20 minutes

⌁ COOKING 15 minutes per tray

⌁ MAKES 12

1 Preheat the oven to 180°C (350°/Gas 4). In a microwave or heavy saucepan over very low heat, melt the butter and chocolate; stir until smooth, then allow to cool.

2 In a large bowl using an electric mixer, beat the eggs until foamy, then gradually beat in the sugar. Dissolve the coffee granules in the boiling water. Add the coffee, vanilla and cooled chocolate mixture to the egg mixture.

3 Combine the flour, salt and baking powder; gradually add to the egg mixture and mix well. Stir in the chocolate chips and nuts.

4 Drop ⅓ cupfuls of the dough 10 cm (4 inches) apart onto ungreased baking trays. Flatten slightly. Bake for about 15 minutes, or until firm. Cool for 4 minutes on the trays, then transfer to a wire rack to cool completely.

CHOC-TOPPED SURPRISE BISCUITS

24 bottled pitted morello cherries,
    drained (reserve 1 tablespoon
    juice)
125 g (4 oz) butter, softened,
    plus ½ teaspoon extra
¾ cup (165 g) firmly packed soft
    brown sugar
1 teaspoon vanilla extract
225 g (8 oz) plain (all-purpose)
    flour
pinch salt
1 cup (170 g) milk chocolate chips

⟶ **PREPARATION** 15 minutes plus chilling
⟶ **COOKING** 17 minutes per tray
⟶ **MAKES** 24

1 Preheat the oven to 180°C (350°F/Gas
4). Pat the cherries with paper towel to
remove excess moisture. In a large bowl
using an electric mixer, beat the butter
and sugar until light and creamy. Beat
in the reserved cherry juice and vanilla.
Sift together the flour and salt; gradually
mix into the creamed mixture. Cover
and refrigerate for 1 hour, or until the
dough is easy to handle.

2 Insert a chocolate chip into each cherry.
Wrap a tablespoon of dough around each
cherry. Place 4 cm (1½ inches) apart on
ungreased baking trays.

3 Bake for 15–17 minutes, or until set and
the edges are lightly browned. Transfer to
wire racks to cool.

4 Melt the remaining chocolate chips
and extra ½ teaspoon butter, and stir
until smooth. Dip the tops of the cooled
biscuits in melted chocolate; allow the
excess to drip off. Place on baking
(parchment) paper and leave until set.

TRIPLE-CHOCOLATE BROWNIE COOKIES

60 g (2 oz) dark chocolate
85 g (3 oz) butter, cubed
2 eggs
1 cup (220 g) sugar
100 g (3½ oz) plain (all-purpose) flour
¼ cup (30 g) unsweetened cocoa
    powder
1 teaspoon baking powder
¼ teaspoon salt
1 cup (170 g) dark chocolate chips
1 teaspoon butter

- PREPARATION 25 minutes plus
    chilling
- COOKING 7–9 minutes per tray
- MAKES 36

1 Preheat the oven to 180°C (350°C/ Gas 4). Melt the chocolate and butter, stir until smooth, and cool slightly. In a large bowl using an electric mixer, beat the eggs and sugar until thick and creamy. Stir in the chocolate mixture. Combine the flour, cocoa, baking powder and salt; gradually add to the chocolate mixture. Stir in ¾ cup (125 g) chocolate chips. Cover and refrigerate for 2 hours, or until easy to handle.

2 Drop level tablespoons of dough about 5 cm (2 inches) apart onto greased baking trays. Bake for 7–9 minutes, or until edges are set and tops are slightly cracked. Cool for 2 minutes then transfer to wire racks to cool completely.

3 In a microwave, melt the remaining chocolate chips and the butter; stir until smooth, then drizzle over cookies. Leave for 30 minutes, or until the chocolate is set. Store in an airtight container.

DOUBLE CHOCOLATE CHUNK AND NUT COOKIES

125 g (4 oz) unsalted butter, softened

⅓ cup (80 g) firmly packed soft brown sugar

½ teaspoon vanilla extract

1 egg, beaten

75 g (2½ oz) white self-raising flour

60 g (2 oz) wholemeal (whole-wheat) plain (all-purpose) flour

2 tablespoons unsweetened cocoa powder

¼ teaspoon baking powder

¼ teaspoon salt

125 g (4 oz) dark chocolate (at least 70 per cent cocoa), roughly chopped

⅓ cup (50 g) macadamia nuts, roughly chopped

3 tablespoons low-fat milk

⁕ PREPARATION 20 minutes

⁕ COOKING 15 minutes per tray

⁕ MAKES 12

1 Preheat the oven to 190°C (375°F/Gas 5). Line 2 baking trays with baking paper.

2 In a large bowl using an electric mixer, beat the butter, sugar and vanilla until light and fluffy. Gradually add the egg, beating well after each addition.

3 Sift the flours, cocoa powder, baking powder and salt over the creamed mixture, tipping in any bran left in the sieve. Add the chocolate, nuts and milk, and mix everything together.

4 Drop tablespoonfuls of the mixture about 5 cm (2 inches) apart onto the prepared baking trays. Flatten slightly with the back of a fork, then bake for about 15 minutes, or until soft and springy.

5 Cool on the baking trays for a few minutes, then transfer to a wire rack. Serve while still slightly warm or leave until cold. Store in an airtight container for up to 5 days.

For a chunky texture, the chocolate and nuts should be chopped in fairly large pieces.

*These cookies are simply irresistible eaten
while still warm, when the chocolate chunks
are still soft and melting.*

CHERRY CHOCOLATE-CHIP COOKIES

1 cup (130 g) dried cherries or
    sweetened dried cranberries,
    chopped
1/3 cup (80 ml) hot water
3/4 cup (185 g) butter
1 1/2 cups (345 g) firmly packed
    soft brown sugar
1/2 cup (115 g) caster (superfine)
    sugar
2 eggs
3 teaspoons grated orange zest
1 1/2 teaspoons vanilla extract
3 cups (300 g) quick-cook
    porridge oats
250 g (8 oz) plain (all-purpose)
    flour
3/4 teaspoon bicarbonate of soda
    (baking soda)
3/4 teaspoon ground cinnamon
1/2 teaspoon salt
1 cup (170 g) dark chocolate chips

·→ PREPARATION 15 minutes
·→ COOKING 12–14 minutes per tray
·→ MAKES 36

1 Preheat the oven to 180°C (350°F/Gas 4). In a
small bowl, soak cherries in hot water for at least
10 minutes. Meanwhile, in a large bowl, cream
butter and sugars until light and fluffy. Beat in
eggs, orange zest and vanilla. Combine oats,
flour, bicarbonate of soda, cinnamon and salt;
gradually mix into creamed mixture. Stir in
chocolate chips, cherries and their soaking liquid.

2 Drop rounded tablespoons of mixture about
5 cm (2 inches) apart onto ungreased baking
trays. Bake for 12–14 minutes, or until the edges
are lightly browned. Cool on the trays for about
2 minutes, then transfer to wire racks.

DOUBLE CHOCOLATE COOKIES

160 g (5½ oz) butter, softened
1 cup (230 g) caster (superfine)
   sugar
1 egg
1 teaspoon vanilla extract
150 g (5 oz) plain (all-purpose) flour
⅓ cup (40 g) unsweetened cocoa
   powder
½ teaspoon bicarbonate of soda
   (baking soda)
¼ teaspoon salt
1 cup (170 g) dark chocolate chips

⁃ **PREPARATION** 10 minutes
⁃ **COOKING** 8–10 minutes per tray
⁃ **MAKES** About 50

When making cookies, it's up to you whether you grease the baking trays, or line them with baking (parchment) paper. If baking multiple batches, you can reuse the same sheet of baking paper for successive trays. Let the trays cool completely between batches, otherwise the cookies may spread too much.

1 Preheat the oven to 180°C (350°F/Gas 4). Grease baking trays. In a large bowl, beat the butter and sugar until combined. Beat in egg and vanilla. Combine flour, cocoa, bicarbonate of soda and salt; gradually mix into the creamed mixture. Stir in the chocolate chips.

2 Drop rounded teaspoons of the dough about 5 cm (2 inches) apart onto the trays. Bake for about 8–10 minutes, or until set. Cool on the trays for 2 minutes, then transfer to wire racks.

CHOCOLATE CHUNK COOKIES

250 g (8 oz) butter

½ cup (115 g) caster (superfine) sugar

½ cup (115 g) firmly packed soft or dark brown sugar

1 egg

1 teaspoon vanilla extract

310 g (11 oz) plain (all-purpose) flour

1 teaspoon bicarbonate of soda (baking soda)

300 g (10 oz) dark chocolate, chopped

•➤ **PREPARATION** 15 minutes

•➤ **COOKING** 12 minutes per tray

•➤ **MAKES** 40

Try milk or white chocolate instead, or a mixture. Roughly chop bars of chocolate if you like large chunks in your cookies, or use packaged chocolate chips.

Dissolve 1 teaspoon instant coffee powder in a little water; add with the egg. Omit the vanilla.

1 Preheat the oven to 180°C (350°F/Gas 4). Grease 2 large baking trays.

2 In a small bowl using an electric mixer, beat the butter and sugars until light and creamy. Beat in the egg and vanilla. Transfer the mixture to a large bowl. Sift the flour and bicarbonate of soda over the mixture, stir to combine, then stir in the chocolate. Roll level tablespoons of dough into balls and place 2.5 cm (1 inch) apart on the prepared trays.

3 Bake for about 12 minutes. Cool briefly on the trays, then transfer to wire racks.

CHOCOLATE NUT COOKIES

Halve the amount of chocolate used and add an equal weight of chopped walnuts, pecans or macadamia nuts. Both chocolate and nuts should be chopped into fairly large pieces.

Toasted nuts give the best flavour. Preheat the oven to 180°C (350°F/Gas 4), spread nuts in a single layer on a baking tray and bake until light golden brown and fragrant. Stir occasionally with a wooden spoon to ensure even browning, and check them frequently, as they burn easily. Allow the nuts to cool before adding them to the cookie dough, or they will melt it.

CHOCOLATE-CHIP OATMEAL COOKIES

With its combination of oats, chocolate chips and peanut butter, this recipe produces cookies that are extra rich and delicious.

125 g (4 oz) unsalted butter, softened
½ cup (125 g) peanut butter
½ cup (110 g) sugar
⅓ cup (80 g) firmly packed soft brown sugar
1 egg
½ teaspoon vanilla extract
125 g (4 oz) plain (all-purpose) flour
½ cup (50 g) quick-cook porridge oats
1 teaspoon bicarbonate of soda (baking soda)
¼ teaspoon salt
1 cup (170 g) dark chocolate chips

·•· PREPARATION 15 minutes
·•· COOKING 10–12 minutes per tray
·•· MAKES 36

1 Preheat the oven to 180°C (350°F/Gas 4).

2 In a large bowl using an electric mixer, beat the butter, peanut butter and sugars until light and creamy. Beat in the egg and vanilla.

3 In a small bowl, combine the flour, oats, bicarbonate of soda and salt.

4 Add the dry ingredients to the creamed mixture and stir until well combined. Stir in the chocolate chips.

5 Drop teaspoonfuls of dough about 5 cm (2 inches) apart onto ungreased baking trays. Bake for 10–12 minutes, or until lightly browned. Cool on the trays for a few minutes, then transfer to wire racks to cool completely.

TRIPLE-CHOCOLATE COOKIES

300 g (10 oz) unsalted butter,
  softened
250 g (8 oz) icing (confectioners')
  sugar
⅓ cup (40 g) unsweetened cocoa
  powder
¼ cup (60 g) sour cream
1 tablespoon vanilla extract
300 g (10 oz) plain (all-purpose)
  flour
2 cups (350 g) dark chocolate
  chips
¼ cup (45 g) chocolate sprinkles

↠ **PREPARATION** 20 minutes plus
  chilling
↠ **COOKING** 10 minutes per tray
↠ **MAKES** About 65

1 In a large bowl using an electric mixer, beat the butter, icing sugar and cocoa until light and creamy. Beat in the sour cream and vanilla.

2 Stir in half the flour and mix well. Add the remaining flour, then stir in the chocolate chips and refrigerate for 1 hour.

3 Preheat oven to 160°C (320°F/Gas 2–3).

4 Roll the chilled dough into 2.5 cm (1 inch) balls. Dip one side of each ball in the sprinkles. Place, sprinkle side up, 5 cm (2 inches) apart on ungreased baking trays. Bake for about 10 minutes, or until set. Cool on the trays for 5 minutes, then transfer to wire racks.

Chocolate chips, chocolate sprinkles and cocoa powder create a triple shot of chocolate flavour. Sour cream makes the cookies irresistibly soft and tender.

CHOCOLATE–ALMOND BISCOTTI

375 g (¾ lb) wholemeal (whole-
     wheat) plain (all-purpose) flour
¾ cup (165 g) sugar
2 teaspoons baking powder
1 teaspoon ground cinnamon
1½ cups whole almonds
175 g (6 oz) dark chocolate,
     chopped
4 large eggs, at room temperature,
     beaten

·→· PREPARATION 20 minutes
·→· COOKING About 1 hour
·→· MAKES About 50

Biscotti is Italian for 'twice-cooked'. This version is packed with almonds, a great source of vitamin E, and drizzled with dark chocolate, which is rich in anti-oxidants. Store the biscotti in an airtight container.

1 Preheat the oven to 180°C (350°F/Gas 4). Line 2 baking trays with baking (parchment) paper. In a large bowl, stir together the flour, sugar, baking powder and cinnamon. Stir in the almonds and 125 g (4 oz) chocolate.

2 Stir the eggs into the flour mixture. Knead the dough on a lightly floured surface until smooth. Cut in half and shape each portion into a log. Place on the prepared trays, flatten slightly and bake for about 30 minutes, or until the outside is puffed and firm. Cool for about 15 minutes.

3 Using a serrated knife, cut the logs crosswise into 1 cm (½ inch) slices. Arrange on the trays in a single layer and bake, turning once, for about 30 minutes, or until crisp. Transfer to wire racks to cool completely.

4 Meanwhile, melt the remaining chocolate in a heatproof bowl set over a saucepan of simmering water. Stir until melted. Drizzle over the biscotti and allow to set.

ESPRESSO BISCOTTI

250 g (8 oz) plain (all-purpose) flour

125 g (4 oz) sugar

¼ cup (30 g) unsweetened cocoa
    powder

3 tablespoons ground coffee beans

1 teaspoon baking powder

¼ teaspoon ground cinnamon

¼ teaspoon salt

85 g (3 oz) unsalted butter, chilled
    and diced

¾ cup (90 g) walnuts

2 eggs, lightly beaten

1 teaspoon vanilla extract

·→· **PREPARATION** 20 minutes

·→· **COOKING** About 45 minutes

·→· **MAKES** About 60

1 Preheat the oven to 180°C (350°F/
Gas 4). Line 2 baking trays with baking
(parchment) paper.

2 In a medium bowl, mix together
the flour, sugar, cocoa, coffee, baking
powder, cinnamon and salt. Add the
butter and beat with an electric mixer
until the mixture resembles coarse meal.
Add the walnuts, eggs, and vanilla and
mix to a fairly dry dough.

3 Knead the dough on a lightly floured
surface until smooth. Cut in half and
shape each portion into a log. Place on
the prepared trays, flatten slightly and
bake for 20–25 minutes, or until the
outside is puffed and firm. Transfer to
wire racks to cool for about 15 minutes.

4 Using a serrated knife, cut the logs
crosswise into 5 mm (¼ inch) slices.
Arrange on the trays in a single layer.
Lower the oven temperature to 150°C
(300°F/Gas 2) and bake for 20 minutes,
turning once. Transfer to wire racks to
cool completely.

PEPPERMINT BISCOTTI

190 g (6½ oz) butter, softened
¾ cup (170 g) sugar
3 eggs, beaten
2 teaspoons peppermint extract
500 g (1 lb) plain (all-purpose) flour
1 teaspoon baking powder
¼ teaspoon salt
1 cup (230 g) crushed peppermint
   candy canes

TOPPING

2 cups (340 g) dark chocolate chips
2 tablespoons butter
½ cup (115 g) crushed peppermint
   candy canes

➺ **PREPARATION** 20 minutes
➺ **COOKING** About 45 minutes
➺ **MAKES** 36

1 Preheat the oven to 180°C (350°F/ Gas 4). In a large bowl using an electric mixer, beat the butter and sugar until light and creamy. Gradually beat in the eggs, a little at a time. Beat in the peppermint extract. Combine the flour, baking powder, salt and crushed candy. Gradually add to the creamed mixture, beating to a stiff dough.

2 Divide dough in half and shape each portion into a log. Place on ungreased baking trays and flatten slightly. Bake for 25–30 minutes, or until golden brown. Cool for about 15 minutes.

3 Using a serrated knife, cut the logs crosswise into 1 cm (½ inch) slices. Arrange on the trays in a single layer and bake, turning once, for about 15 minutes, or until crisp. Transfer to wire racks to cool.

4 Melt chocolate chips and butter; stir until smooth. Drizzle over biscotti then sprinkle them with crushed candy. Place on baking (parchment) paper until set.

DOUBLE CHOCOLATE BISCOTTI

*T*hese biscotti are a slightly softer and a little
more moist than usual. They go particularly
well with a cup of hot coffee.

2 eggs

1 teaspoon vanilla extract

¼ teaspoon almond extract

½ cup (110 g) sugar

150 g (5 oz) plain (all-purpose)
flour

½ cup (60 g) finely chopped
pecans

¼ cup (30 g) unsweetened cocoa
powder

¼ teaspoon salt

½ cup (85 g) dark chocolate chips

···→ PREPARATION 10 minutes

···→ COOKING About 4 minutes

···→ MAKES 12–15

1 Preheat the oven to 180°C (350°F/Gas 4).
Grease a large baking tray.

2 In a large bowl using an electric mixer, beat
the eggs, vanilla and almond extract until
combined. Beat in the sugar. Combine the flour,
pecans, cocoa and salt; gradually add to the egg
mixture. Stir in the chocolate chips.

3 Shape the dough into a log and place on the
prepared tray. Bake for 20–25 minutes, or until
lightly browned. Cool for about 15 minutes.

4 Using a serrated knife, cut crosswise into
2.5 cm (1 inch) slices. Arrange on baking trays
and bake for 15–20 minutes, or until firm.
Transfer to a wire rack to cool.

CHOCOLATE MACADAMIA MACAROONS

2 cups (110 g) flaked coconut

½ cup (70 g) finely chopped macadamia nuts

⅓ cup (80 g) caster (superfine) sugar

¼ cup (30 g) unsweetened cocoa powder

2 tablespoons plain (all-purpose) flour

1 pinch salt

2 eggwhites, beaten

1 tablespoon light corn syrup

1 teaspoon vanilla extract

¾ cup (110 g) roughly chopped dark chocolate

⁓ **PREPARATION** 20 minutes

⁓ **COOKING** 15–20 minutes

⁓ **MAKES** 18

1 Preheat the oven to 160°C (320°F/Gas 2–3). Grease 2 baking trays. In a large bowl, combine the coconut, macadamia nuts, sugar, cocoa, flour and salt. Add the eggwhites, corn syrup and vanilla and mix well.

2 Drop rounded tablespoons of dough about 5 cm (2 inches) apart onto the prepared trays. Bake for 15–20 minutes, or until set and dry to the touch. Cool on the trays for 5 minutes, then transfer to wire racks to cool completely.

3 In a microwave, melt the chocolate; stir until smooth. Dip the bottom of each macaroon in the chocolate, allowing the excess to drip off. Place on baking (parchment) paper; let stand until set.

If you can't find light corn syrup, use golden syrup or honey.

Full of coconut and macadamia nuts, these macaroons are easy to make. They're dipped in chocolate for extra appeal.

CHOCOLATE MACARONS

¾ cup (90 g) almond meal
  (ground almonds)
200 g (7 oz) icing
  (confectioners') sugar
25 g (2½ tablespoons)
  Dutch cocoa powder
3 large eggwhites
¼ cup (55 g) caster
  (superfine) sugar

CHOCOLATE FILLING
150 ml (5 fl oz) thickened (heavy/
  double) whipping cream
200 g (7 oz) dark chocolate,
  finely chopped

·→ PREPARATION 15 minutes
    plus resting
·→ COOKING 20 minutes
·→ MAKES About 20

French-style 'macarons' such as these are a mixture of eggwhite and ground nuts (usually almonds), sandwiched together with a flavoured filling, while the main ingredients of 'macaroons' are eggwhite and coconut.

1 Preheat the oven to 150°C (300°F/Gas 2). Line 2 baking trays with baking (parchment) paper.

2 In a large bowl using an electric mixer, beat the almond meal, icing sugar and cocoa on low speed until combined. Pass the mixture through a sieve onto baking paper.

3 Whisk eggwhites until foamy. While beating, gradually add the caster sugar and beat until soft peaks form and the sugar is dissolved. Using a rubber spatula, gently fold the almond mixture into the eggwhites, one-third at a time.

4 Transfer the mixture to a piping (icing) bag fitted with a 1 cm (½ inch) plain nozzle. Pipe 4 cm (1½ inch) rounds onto the prepared trays, allowing room for spreading. Leave to rest for 30–60 minutes to allow a skin to form.

5 Bake for 20 minutes, or until puffed, firm to touch and crusted a little. Cool for 10–15 minutes on the trays, then transfer to wire racks.

6 For the filling, bring cream to a boil in a small saucepan. Remove from heat, add the chocolate and stand 2 minutes. Stir until smooth. Let stand at room temperature or chill for 10 minutes until the mixture is spreadable. Sandwich cooled macarons together with the filling.

SWEET TREATS AND DRINKS

DOUBLE-DECKER PALMIERS

300 g (10 oz) frozen puff or flaky
   pastry sheets
100 g (3½ oz) sugar
plain (all-purpose) flour, for dusting
100 g (3½ oz) milk chocolate

FILLING
200 ml (7 fl oz) cream, for whipping
1 tablespoon puréed red jam
   (such as cherry, strawberry,
   raspberry or currant)

·•· PREPARATION 25 minutes
·•· COOKING 16–18 minutes per tray
·•· MAKES 35–40 individual pastries
     or 18–20 pastry sandwiches

1 Place the pastry sheets in a single
layer on a lightly floured surface; allow
to thaw.

2 Preheat the oven to 180°C (350°F/
Gas 4). Line 2 baking trays with baking
(parchment) paper.

3 Stack the pastry sheets one on top of
the other, sprinkling each sheet with
sugar as you go, including the top layer.

4 Roll out the stack of pastry sheets to
make a rectangle about 25 x 40 cm
(10 x 16 inches). Sprinkle with more sugar.

5 Roll the dough up from each long side until they meet in the middle. Using a sharp knife, cut into slices about 5 mm (¼ inch) thick. Place the pastries about 5 cm (2 inches) apart on the prepared trays. Bake each tray in the centre of the oven for 16–18 minutes, or until the pastries are golden brown.

6 Meanwhile, melt the chocolate. Remove palmiers from oven and transfer to wire racks; let cool. Set half of them aside for spreading. Dip the tips of the remaining pastries in the chocolate; leave to set.

7 To make the filling, beat the cream until almost stiff. Fold in enough fruit spread to turn the cream pink, then beat until stiff.

8 Pipe the cream mixture onto the pastries using an icing (piping) bag fitted with a plain nozzle, or simply spread it on with a spoon. Sandwich with the chocolate-tipped pastries. Serve at once.

The cream will remain stable for longer if you add a cream stiffener or instant gelatin (follow the directions on the packet). The palmiers also taste good on their own, without the chocolate and filling. If you are serving them plain, mix a little cinnamon into the sugar.

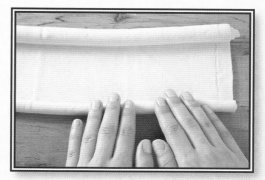

Roll up the long sides of the pastry towards the middle, until the two rolls meet.

To make the palmier shape, use a sharp knife to cut the rolled-up pastry sheets into slices.

Once the palmiers have been baked and cooled, dip half the biscuits in the melted chocolate.

CHOCOLATE WHOOPIE PIES

125 g (4 oz) butter, softened
¾ cup (170 g) caster (superfine)
   sugar
1 egg
1 teaspoon vanilla extract
300 g (10 oz) plain (all-purpose)
   flour
⅓ cup (40 g) unsweetened cocoa
   powder
1 teaspoon bicarbonate of soda
   (baking soda)
¼ teaspoon salt
¾ cup (180 ml) buttermilk

FILLING
1 cup (100 g) white marshmallows
60 g (2 oz) butter, softened
1 teaspoon vanilla extract
1 cup (125 g) icing
   (confectioners') sugar

•• PREPARATION 15 minutes
•• COOKING 5–7 minutes per tray
•• MAKES 15

1 Preheat the oven to 190°C (375°F/Gas 5).
Grease 2 baking trays.

2 In a large bowl using an electric mixer, beat
the butter and sugar until light and creamy.
Beat in the egg and vanilla. Combine the flour,
cocoa, bicarbonate of soda and salt; add to the
creamed mixture alternately with ¼ cup (60 ml)
water and the buttermilk, beating well after each
addition.

3 Drop tablespoonfuls of mixture 5 cm (2 inches)
apart onto the trays. Bake for 5–7 minutes, or until
set. Transfer to wire racks to cool completely.

4 To make the filling, melt the marshmallows in
the microwave for 8–10 seconds. Set aside to cool
to room temperature. In a small bowl using an
electric mixer, beat the butter and vanilla until
fluffy. Beat in the marshmallows and icing sugar
and beat well until thick. Spread on the flat sides
of half of the cookies; sandwich with the
remaining cookies.

Chocolate lovers will find these cute goodies irresistible. Two luscious cakey-textured cookies encase a soft marshmallow filling.

CHOCOLATE PRETZELS

250 g (8 oz) butter, softened
400 g (14 oz) icing (confectioners')
 sugar
1 whole egg and 1 egg yolk
350 g (12 oz) plain (all-purpose) flour
2–3 tablespoons unsweetened cocoa
 powder
1 tablespoon butter
2 tablespoons boiling water, or as
 needed

⇥ **PREPARATION** 35 minutes
⇥ **COOKING** 10–15 minutes per tray
⇥ **MAKES** 100

1 Preheat oven to 200°C (400°F/Gas 6). Cut pieces of baking (parchment) paper to fit 2 large baking trays (or more if you have them). Using a template or a cookie cutter, draw pretzel shapes onto the paper. Place the paper onto the trays.

2 In a large bowl using an electric mixer, beat the butter until fluffy. Add 100 g (3½ oz) icing sugar and the combined egg and egg yolk; stir to combine. Sift the flour over the mixture and stir in.

3 Spoon dough into a piping (icing) bag fitted with a small, round, plain nozzle. Following the drawn outlines, pipe the dough onto the prepared trays. Bake, one tray at a time, for 10–15 minutes, or until golden. Transfer to wire racks to cool.

4 To make a glaze, combine the remaining icing sugar with the cocoa, butter and about 2 tablespoons boiling water. Dip pretzels in the glaze and place on wire racks covered with foil to dry.

PIPED ALMOND CIRCLES

250 g (8 oz) butter, softened
200 g (7 oz) sugar
2 egg yolks
1 tablespoon rum
1½ cups (150 g) almond meal (ground almonds)
350 g (12 oz) plain (all-purpose) flour
2–3 tablespoons milk
150 g (5 oz) dark chocolate

⌁ PREPARATION 45 minutes
⌁ COOKING 12–15 minutes per tray
⌁ MAKES 70

⌘ The dough must be just soft enough so that the cookies can easily be shaped with a piping (icing) bag.

1 Preheat the oven to 180°C (350°F/Gas 4). Line 2 large baking trays with baking (parchment) paper.

2 In a large bowl using an electric mixer, beat the butter, sugar, egg yolks and rum until light and creamy. Combine the almond meal and flour and stir in alternately with the milk.

3 Spoon the dough into a piping (icing) bag with a star nozzle. Pipe circles of dough about 2.5 cm (1 inch) apart onto the prepared trays. (The cookies should not be too thin or they will be more likely to break later). Bake, one tray at a time, for 12–15 minutes, or until golden. Cool on the trays for a few minutes, then transfer to wire racks to cool completely.

4 Melt the chocolate in a heatproof bowl set over a saucepan of gently simmering water. Dip one half of each cookie into the melted chocolate. Place on sheets of baking paper and leave to set and dry.

PROFITEROLES WITH CHOCOLATE SAUCE

85 g (3 oz) plain (all-purpose) flour
pinch salt
60 g (2 oz) butter
2 whole eggs and 1 egg yolk
1 cup (250 ml) cream, for whipping

CHOCOLATE SAUCE

200 g (7 oz) dark chocolate,
    chopped
30 g (1 oz) butter, chopped

- **PREPARATION** 15 minutes
- **COOKING** 20–30 minutes plus drying
- **MAKES** 12 large or 15 small
    profiteroles

1 Preheat the oven to 220°C (425°F/ Gas 7). Lightly grease a baking tray.

2 To make the pastry, sift the flour and salt onto a sheet of baking (parchment) paper. Heat 1/2 cup (125 ml) water and the butter in a saucepan until the butter is melted and the water just begins to boil. Remove from the heat, tip the flour quickly into the saucepan and beat the mixture with a wooden spoon until

smooth. Return briefly to the heat and continue beating until the mixture binds together and comes away from the side of the pan. Remove from the heat and allow to cool for 1 minute.

3 Break one egg into the saucepan and beat the pastry well with the wooden spoon. Add the other egg and the yolk and beat again until the pastry is glossy.

4 Place rounded tablespoons of the warm mixture at least 2.5 cm (1 inch) apart on the prepared tray. Bake for 20–30 minutes, until well puffed up and golden — do not open the oven door for the first 20 minutes.

5 Turn the heat off and leave the puffs in the oven for about 30 minutes, with the door ajar, to dry completely. They are best eaten fresh, but can be baked ahead and stored in an airtight container for a day.

6 Make the filling and fill the puffs just before serving. Whip the cream, then spoon it into a piping (icing) bag

fitted with a plain nozzle. Use the nozzle to pierce a hole in each puff and fill it generously with cream. Or, gently cut each puff in half, pipe cream into the bottom half and replace the top. Divide among individual bowls or plates.

7 For the chocolate sauce, combine the chocolate, butter and 3 tablespoons water in a heatproof bowl set over a saucepan of medium–hot (not simmering) water. Stir until the sauce is melted and smooth. Spoon liberally over the profiteroles and serve immediately.

CHOCOLATE AND COFFEE ÉCLAIRS

FILLING

2½ cups (625 ml) low-fat milk

1 vanilla bean, halved lengthwise

3 teaspoons ground coffee beans

60 g (2 oz) cornflour (cornstarch)

2½ tablespoons sugar

150 g (5 oz) low-fat Greek-style
   yogurt

CHOUX PASTRY

85 g (3 oz) low-fat spread

125 g (4 oz) plain (all-purpose)
   flour

2 whole eggs plus 1 eggwhite

ICING

100 g (3½ oz) dark chocolate

2 teaspoons icing (confectioners')
   sugar, sifted

··• PREPARATION 45 minutes plus
     infusing and chilling

··• COOKING 30 minutes

··• MAKES 20

1 To make the filling, combine the milk, vanilla bean and ground coffee in a saucepan and bring to a boil. Remove from the heat, cover with a tight-fitting lid and leave to infuse for 1 hour.

2 Meanwhile, make the pastry. Line 2 baking trays with baking (parchment) paper and set aside. Pour ¾ cup (180 ml) water into a saucepan, add the spread and cover the pan. Heat gently until the spread has melted, then uncover the pan and bring to a boil.

3 Remove the pan from the heat and stir in the flour. Return to the heat and stir until the mixture forms a ball in the centre of the pan and leaves the side clean. Remove from the heat and allow the mixture to cool for 2–3 minutes.

4 Beat the whole eggs and eggwhite together with a fork. Using an electric mixer, beat the egg mixture into the cooled pastry mixture a little at a time, beating well between additions, until the mixture is smooth and shiny and will hold a soft peak.

5 Spoon the pastry into a large piping (icing) bag fitted with a 1 cm (½ inch) plain nozzle. Pipe onto the prepared trays in straight lengths about 10 cm (4 inches) long, spacing them 2.5 cm (1 inch) apart. Cut the pastry cleanly away from the end of the nozzle with a knife.

6 Freeze the piped pastry, uncovered, for 30 minutes, or until firm. Then cover with foil and return to the freezer.

7 Meanwhile, continue making the filling: line a sieve with muslin (cheesecloth) or paper towels and strain the infused milk into a jug (pitcher), discarding the vanilla bean and coffee grounds.

8 Put the cornflour and sugar into a saucepan, gradually stir in the strained milk and bring to a boil, stirring continuously. The mixture will be lumpy to start with, but will thicken and become smooth as it reaches a boil. Reduce the heat to low and cook for a further 2–3 minutes, stirring. Pour the filling into a bowl, cover with plastic wrap and leave to cool. Chill for 3 hours, or overnight, for the filling to set.

9 When the filling has set, heat the oven to 220°C (425°F/Gas 7) and bake the choux pastry from frozen for 25 minutes, or until well risen, golden brown and crisp. Remove the éclairs from the oven. Pierce each éclair at one end to allow the steam to escape, then return them to the turned-off oven for 5 minutes to dry out completely. Transfer to wire racks to cool.

10 To make the icing, bring a small saucepan half full of water to simmering point. Put ⅓ cup (80 ml) water, the chocolate and the icing sugar in a small heatproof bowl set over the pan of water and stir until the mixture is smooth.

11 To fill the cooled éclairs, whisk the chilled filling until smooth, then fold in the yogurt. Spoon the mixture into a large piping (icing) bag fitted with a 1 cm (½ inch) star nozzle.

12 Using a serrated knife, carefully slice the top third off each éclair. Pipe the filling generously along the base of each, then replace the tops and return the éclairs to the wire racks.

13 Spoon the chocolate icing along the top of each éclair, allowing it to trickle a little down the sides, and leave in a cool place until set. The éclairs can be kept, covered, in the refrigerator for 3–4 hours before serving. They are best eaten on the day they are made.

If you don't want a coffee flavour in the filling, you can infuse the milk with two vanilla beans instead.

CHOCOLATE TRUFFLES

200 ml (7 fl oz) thickened (heavy/
    double) whipping cream
300 g (10 oz) dark chocolate,
    finely chopped
30 g (1 oz) unsalted butter
1 tablespoon brandy or liqueur,
    such as Grand Marnier or
    Frangelico
200 g (7 oz) Dutch cocoa powder

- **PREPARATION** 15 minutes plus
    overnight chilling
- **COOKING** Nil
- **MAKES** 30

These truffles are simply
a chocolate ganache dusted
with cocoa powder. For greatest
enjoyment, eat them cold, not
warm. You will need to begin
this recipe the day before.

1 Bring the cream gently to a boil in a saucepan.
Remove from the heat and add the chocolate.
Stand for 2–3 minutes, then stir to combine.
Add the butter and liqueur and stir with a rubber
spatula until the mixture is glossy and smooth.

2 Scrape down the sides of the bowl and cover
with plastic wrap, pressing down to prevent air
from coming into contact with the chocolate.
Refrigerate overnight to firm.

3 The next day, line a baking tray with baking
(parchment) paper and sift the cocoa over it.
Using a metal spoon, a piping (icing) bag or a
small ice-cream scoop, drop small amounts of
the mixture onto the cocoa and roll the balls
until covered. (Move them about with a fork or
spoon rather than your hands, so the chocolate
does not melt.)

4 Place on a tray lined with baking paper.
Refrigerate for 2–3 hours, or until firm.

*These little chocolate explosions are rich, dark
and lightly flavoured with liqueur.*

QUICK CHOCOLATE TRUFFLES

3 cups (500 g) dark chocolate
   chips
400 g (14 oz) can sweetened
   condensed milk
1 tablespoon vanilla extract
desiccated coconut, chocolate
   sprinkles, coloured sprinkles,
   unsweetened cocoa powder
   and/or finely chopped nuts,
   to decorate (optional)

PREPARATION 20 minutes plus
   chilling
COOKING Nil
MAKES 48

1 In a microwave-safe bowl, melt the chocolate chips and condensed milk on low–medium power; stir until smooth. Stir in the vanilla. Chill for 2 hours, or until mixture is easy to handle.

2 Using a metal teaspoon, shape into 2.5 cm (1 inch) balls. Roll in coconut, sprinkles, cocoa or nuts if desired. Store in an airtight container in the refrigerator.

For an attractive presentation, roll a few truffles in each of the different coatings.

These smooth, creamy chocolates are divine. And, with just a few ingredients, they're quick and easy to make.

FESTIVE TRUFFLES

*T*he week before Christmas, spend some time baking a selection of goodies for friends and family. These little treats couldn't be easier.

250 (8 oz) cream cheese, softened
3 cups (375 g) icing (confectioners') sugar
350 g (12 oz) dark chocolate, chopped
1½ teaspoons vanilla extract
¾ cup each crushed peppermint candy, flaked coconut and chopped or ground nuts

- PREPARATION 45 minutes plus chilling
- COOKING Nil
- MAKES 60

Truffles are normally made with dark chocolate for the richest flavour, but you can use milk or white chocolate if you prefer. This recipe includes cream cheese rather than the usual cream.

1 In a large bowl using an electric mixer, beat the cream cheese until fluffy. Gradually beat in icing sugar until smooth.

2 In a microwave, melt the chocolate; stir until smooth. Add the chocolate and vanilla to the cream cheese mixture and beat until blended. Cover and refrigerate for 1 hour.

3 Using a small metal spoon, shape into 2.5 cm (1 inch) balls. Roll in crushed peppermint candy, coconut or nuts. Store in an airtight container in the refrigerator.

CHOCOLATE-DIPPED TRUFFLES

FILLING

150 ml (5 fl oz) thickened (heavy/
double) whipping cream
350 g (12 oz) dark chocolate,
chilled then finely grated
60 g (2 oz) unsalted butter, diced
1–2 tablespoons liqueur (optional)

COATING AND DECORATION

350 g (12 oz) dark chocolate
unsweetened cocoa powder,
for dusting,
white chocolate, for drizzling
thin sheets of gold leaf, to
decorate

⁘ **PREPARATION** 45 minutes plus
chilling and freezing
⁘ **COOKING** Nil
⁘ **MAKES** About 35

1 Bring the cream to a boil in a small saucepan. Remove from the heat and add the grated chocolate and butter. Stir constantly until the mixture is thick, dark and smooth. Add the liqueur if using, then transfer the mixture to a small bowl. Scrape down the side of the bowl and cover with plastic wrap, pressing down to prevent air from coming into contact with the chocolate mixture. Refrigerate until quite firm.

2 Using a metal teaspoon, shape the mixture into 2.5 cm (1 inch) balls. Place on a tray lined with baking (parchment) paper and freeze until solid.

3 Melt the remaining chocolate, then remove half the truffles from the freezer and, using a fork, dip them one by one into the chocolate. Shake off the excess and place the truffles on a tray lined with baking paper. Dip the remaining truffles.

4 For a contrast of smooth and soft surfaces, roll some of the truffles in cocoa straight away, before the coating has fully set. Leave the rest to set completely. Then pipe a little melted white chocolate onto some of them and, using your fingertip, press a little gold leaf onto others. Store in an airtight container in the refrigerator for up to 2 weeks, or they can be frozen for a month.

Made from the finest chocolate and decorated with real gold, truffles are the ultimate after-dinner luxury.

TWO-TIERED FUDGE

CHOCOLATE NUT LAYER

2 tablespoons butter, plus
    2 teaspoons extra for greasing
450 g (1 lb) sugar
1 cup (250 ml) milk
85 g (3 oz) dark chocolate
1 tablespoon light corn syrup
    or golden syrup
1 teaspoon vanilla extract
½ cup (60 g) chopped nuts

CHERRY VANILLA LAYER

2 tablespoons butter, plus
    1 teaspoon extra for greasing
450 g (1 lb) sugar
½ cup (125 ml) thickened (heavy/
    double) whipping cream
½ cup (125 ml) milk
1 tablespoon light corn syrup
    or golden syrup
¼ teaspoon salt
1 teaspoon vanilla extract
⅓ cup (80 g) chopped glacé
    (candied) cherries

⋅•‣ PREPARATION 30 minutes
⋅•‣ COOKING Nil
⋅•‣ MAKES About 1.25 kg (2½ lb)

1 Line a 23 cm (9 inch) square cake tin with foil, allowing the foil to overhang on two opposite sides for easy removal. Grease the foil with 1 teaspoon butter.

2 For the chocolate nut layer, butter the inside of a large heavy-based saucepan with 1 teaspoon butter. Add the sugar, milk, chocolate and corn syrup. Cook, stirring, over medium heat until the sugar is dissolved. Bring to a boil and boil, stirring occasionally, until the mixture reaches 112–116°C (234–236°F), or soft-ball stage, on a sugar (candy) thermometer. Remove from heat.

3 Add vanilla and remaining butter (do not stir). Cool to 43°C (110°F) without stirring. Stir with a clean dry wooden spoon until fudge begins to thicken; add nuts. Stir for a further 10 minutes, or until fudge becomes thick and begins to lose its gloss. Immediately pour into the prepared tin.

4 For the cherry vanilla layer, butter the inside of a large clean heavy-based saucepan with 1 teaspoon butter. Add the sugar, cream, milk, corn syrup and salt. Cook, stirring, over medium heat until the sugar is dissolved. Bring to a boil and boil, stirring occasionally, until the mixture reaches 112–116°C (234–236°F), or soft-ball stage. Remove from heat.

5 Add vanilla and remaining butter (do not stir). Cool to 43°C (110°F) without stirring. Stir with a wooden spoon until fudge begins to thicken; add cherries. Continue stirring for about 8 minutes, or until the fudge becomes thick and begins to lose its gloss. Immediately pour it over the first layer.

6 Score into squares while still warm. Cool in the tin, then lift the fudge out of the tin. Discard foil; cut fudge into 2.5 cm (1 inch) squares. Store in an airtight container at room temperature.

Fudge can be tricky, but the flavour of this recipe proves that the results are worth it! Not to mention the sense of achievement …

Stirring fudge

🍂 Allow the fudge to cool to 43°C (110°F) undisturbed. Agitating it at this stage may cause the fudge to become grainy. Once it reaches 43°C (110°F), beat it with a clean dry wooden spoon. As you stir the fudge, the temperature will continue to drop and the mixture will start to become thick and harder to stir.

🍂 As you continue to stir, the fudge will thicken. It may also have paler streaks in it, and it starts to lose its gloss. This step could take up to 10 minutes.

🍂 Once the fudge starts to lose its sheen, immediately pour it into the tin.

Once the fudge reaches 43°C (110°F), beat it with a clean dry wooden spoon.

🍂 Determining the point at which the fudge is ready to pour is important to its success. If it is poured too soon it will be soft; if stirred too much, it will be grainy or will set in the saucepan.

MACADAMIA FUDGE

1½ teaspoons butter, softened
3 cups (500 g) dark chocolate
  chips
400 g (14 oz) can sweetened
  condensed milk
pinch salt
1 cup (135 g) chopped
  macadamia nuts
1½ teaspoons vanilla extract

→ **PREPARATION** 15 minutes plus
  chilling
→ **COOKING** Nil
→ **MAKES** about 1 kg (2 lb)

1 Line a 20 cm (8 inch) square cake tin with foil, allowing foil to overhang on two opposite sides for easy removal. Grease the foil with butter.

2 In a heavy saucepan or in a heatproof bowl set over a saucepan of simmering water, combine the chocolate chips, condensed milk and salt. Cook, stirring, over low heat until the chocolate is melted. Remove from the heat; stir in the macadamia nuts and vanilla. Pour into the prepared tin and chill for 2 hours, or until firm.

3 Score into squares while still warm. Cool in the tin, then lift the fudge out of the tin. Discard foil; cut fudge into 2.5 cm (1 inch) squares. Store in an airtight container at room temperature.

ꙮ This is a quick and easy fudge recipe. Unlike others, it doesn't require precise timing or a sugar (candy) thermometer.

*The creaminess of macadamia nuts is perfect
in this rich fudge, but substitute walnuts,
pecans or almonds if you prefer.*

CHOCOLATE CRACKLES

1 cup (125 g) icing (confectioners')
    sugar
4 tablespoons (50 g) unsweetened
    cocoa powder
4 cups (120 g) puffed rice cereal, such
    as Rice Bubbles or Rice Krispies
1 cup (120 g) desiccated coconut
250 g (8 oz) solid white vegetable
    shortening, such as Copha,
    Kremalta, Trex or Crisco,
    chopped

--- PREPARATION 15 minutes plus chilling
--- COOKING Nil
--- MAKES 24

1 Line two 12-hole standard (⅓ cup/80 ml)
muffin tins or cupcake pans with paper
cases, or use silicone moulds.

2 Sift the icing sugar and cocoa into a
large bowl. Add the puffed rice cereal
and coconut and mix to combine.

3 Melt the shortening in a small saucepan
over low heat. Do not boil. Allow to cool
slightly. Add melted shortening to the
cereal mixture. Mix well.

4 Spoon about 2 teaspoons mixture
into each paper case and chill until firm.

Whether you call them chocolate
crackles or rice krispy treats, these
crunchy confections are a party-time
favourite for everyone.

For a pure chocolate version, omit
sugar, cocoa and shortening. Melt 200 g
(7 oz) milk chocolate and 100 g (3½ oz)
dark chocolate. Gently stir in 3 cups
(90 g) puffed rice cereal and 1 cup
(120 g) desiccated coconut. Spoon into
paper cases and refrigerate until firm.

CHOCOLATE ROASTED NUT SLICE

300 g (10 oz) dark chocolate, melted

1 cup (140 g) toasted hazelnuts, skin removed

1 cup (100 g) toasted walnuts or 1 cup (150 g) blanched almonds

30 g (1 oz) dried apricots, finely sliced

½ teaspoon ground ginger

⤜ **PREPARATION** 10 minutes plus chilling

⤜ **COOKING** Nil

⤜ **MAKES** 20

1 Line a baking tray with baking (parchment) paper.

2 In a bowl, stir together the chocolate, nuts, apricots and ground ginger until smooth and combined. Pour onto the tray to form a rough oblong shape about 15 x 25 cm (6 x 10 inches).

3 Smooth the top with a spatula and refrigerate for 1 hour, or until set.

4 Using a sharp knife, cut into finger lengths and store in an airtight container.

Try this with other combinations of nuts and fruit, such as pecans and dried cherries, or pistachios and sweetened dried cranberries.

CHOC–NUT BARK

2 cups (460 g) caster (superfine) sugar

½ cup (70 g) pistachios, toasted and coarsely chopped

½ cup (40 g) flaked almonds, toasted

200 g (7 oz) dark chocolate, melted

·→· **PREPARATION** 20 minutes plus chilling

·→· **COOKING** Nil

·→· **MAKES** 16

1 Line a baking tray with baking (parchment) paper.

2 Place the sugar and ½ cup (125 ml) water in a medium saucepan over low heat. Cook, stirring, without boiling, for 2–3 minutes, or until the sugar has dissolved. Increase the heat to medium and bring to a boil. Boil, without stirring, for 6–8 minutes, or until the toffee is a deep golden colour. Remove from the heat and allow the bubbles to subside. Stir in the nuts and pour the mixture onto the prepared tray, allowing it to flow into a freeform shape. Stand for about 1 hour, or until set.

3 Turn the toffee slab over and peel away the baking paper. Spread the melted chocolate over the flat side of the toffee. Refrigerate for 10 minutes, or until the chocolate sets. Break into 16 pieces. Store in an airtight container in a cool, dry place for up to 4 days.

These nuggets of chocolate-coated nut toffee are lovely with an after-dinner coffee, or wrapped with a pretty ribbon and given as gifts.

CHOC–MINT CUPS

*U*sing paper mini muffin cases to form your own chocolates is easy, and helps to give them an impressively professional look.

200 g (7 oz) dark chocolate, melted
¼ cup (60 ml) thickened (heavy/ double) whipping cream
200 g (7 oz) dark chocolate, chopped
1 tablespoon peppermint liqueur (optional)
2 x 35 g (1 oz) peppermint crisp chocolate bars, finely chopped

••• PREPARATION 30 minutes plus chilling
••• COOKING Nil
••• MAKES 30

1 Using a small clean pastry brush or paint brush, brush the melted chocolate thickly inside 30 paper mini muffin cases (2.5 cm/1 inch across the base and 4 cm/1½ inches across the top). Place on a tray and refrigerate for 30 minutes, or until set.

2 Combine the cream and chopped chocolate in a small saucepan over low heat. Stir until melted and smooth. Transfer the mixture to a small bowl. Cool for 10 minutes. Stir in the liqueur (if using) and ¾ of the peppermint crisp. Cool for a further 10 minutes.

3 Spoon the mixture into the chocolate cases. Sprinkle the tops with the remaining peppermint crisp. Refrigerate for 3 hours, or until firm. Peel away and discard the paper cases. Store the chocolates in an airtight container in the fridge or a cool, dry place for up to 1 week.

CHOCOLATE-DIPPED CARAMELS

400 g (14 oz) can sweetened
  condensed milk
1 cup (230 g) firmly packed dark
  brown sugar
125 g (4 oz) unsalted butter,
  chopped
350 g (12 oz) milk chocolate
1 teaspoon vegetable oil

•→ **PREPARATION** 20 minutes
•→ **COOKING** 20 minutes plus chilling
•→ **MAKES** 64

🌀 Use a heavy-based saucepan
and stir the caramel continuously
to prevent it from sticking to the
base and burning. Do not bring
the caramel to a boil until the
sugar is fully dissolved. Boiling
the mixture with undissolved
sugar will cause it to crystallise.

🌀 For salted caramels, sprinkle
two or three sea salt flakes on
each caramel after coating them
with the melted chocolate.

1 Grease a 20 cm (8 inch) square cake tin. Line
the base and sides with baking (parchment)
paper, extending the paper over two opposite
sides for easy removal.

2 Put the condensed milk, sugar and butter in a
medium saucepan over low heat. Cook, stirring,
without boiling, for 3–4 minutes, or until sugar
has dissolved. Increase heat to medium. Bring to
a boil, stirring, and continue to stir constantly for
8–10 minutes, or until mixture thickens and turns
a deep caramel colour. Remove from the heat.

3 Pour caramel into prepared tin. Smooth the
top with a hot knife or spatula. Stand at room
temperature for 30 minutes, or until the surface
is set. Using a sharp knife, score the surface into
64 squares. Cover and refrigerate for 6 hours or
until firm. Using a hot knife, cut into squares.

4 Combine the chocolate and oil in a heatproof
bowl set over a saucepan of simmering water.
Stir until melted and smooth. Cool for 5 minutes.
Using a fork, dip the caramels in the melted
chocolate. Place on wire racks set over a tray.
Refrigerate for 30 minutes, or until set. Store the
chocolates in an airtight container in the fridge
or a cool, dry place for up to 1 week.

CHOCOLATE, CHERRY AND COCONUT BITES

250 g (8 oz) glacé (candied)
   cherries
150 g (5 oz) dried mixed berries
   (see note)
1½ cups (120 g) desiccated
   coconut
1 cup (50 g) shredded coconut
1½ cups (185 g) icing
   (confectioners') sugar
½ cup (175 g) sweetened
   condensed milk
1 eggwhite
400 g (14 oz) dark chocolate
1½ teaspoons vegetable oil

•┅• PREPARATION 20 minutes plus
   chilling
•┅• COOKING Nil
•┅• MAKES About 50

🖎 Dried mixed berries are a
combination of dried cranberries,
strawberries and blueberries. Look
for them in large supermarkets.
They can be replaced with dried
cherries or dried cranberries.

1 Line the base and two long sides of a 17 x
28 cm (6½ x 11 inch) baking tin with baking
(parchment) paper. Process the cherries and
dried berries in a food processor for 30 seconds,
or until finely chopped. Add the desiccated and
shredded coconut, sugar, condensed milk and
eggwhite and process for 30 seconds, or until
combined.

2 Press into the prepared tin. Smooth the top
with a hot knife or spatula. Cover and refrigerate
for 6 hours, or until just firm. Using a sharp
knife, cut into 50 rectangles, each about 2.5 x
4 cm (1 x 1½ inches).

3 Combine the chocolate and oil in a heatproof
bowl set over a saucepan of simmering water.
Stir until melted and smooth. Cool for 5 minutes.
Using a fork, dip the cherry bites in the melted
chocolate. Place on wire racks set over a tray.
Refrigerate for 30 minutes, or until set. Store the
chocolates in an airtight container in the fridge
or a cool, dry place for up to 1 week.

Soft-centred hazelnut chocolates

¼ cup (60 ml) thickened (heavy/
  double) whipping cream
2 tablespoons hazelnut liqueur,
  such as Frangelico
200 g (7 oz) milk chocolate,
  chopped
⅓ cup (40 g) finely chopped
  roasted hazelnuts
250 g (8 oz) dark chocolate,
  chopped

- **PREPARATION** 30 minutes plus
  chilling
- **COOKING** Nil
- **MAKES** 30

Store in an airtight container
in the refrigerator or in a cool, dry
place for up to 1 week.

1 Combine the cream, liqueur and milk
chocolate in a small saucepan over low heat.
Stir until melted and smooth. Remove from
the heat and transfer the mixture to small bowl.
Stir in ¼ cup of the chopped hazelnuts. Cover
and refrigerate for 3 hours.

2 Working with a quarter of the chocolate
mixture at a time (keeping the remainder in the
refrigerator), roll rounded teaspoonfuls of the
mixture into balls. Place on a tray lined with
baking (parchment) paper and refrigerate for
2 hours, or until firm.

3 Melt the dark chocolate in a heatproof bowl
over a saucepan of barely simmering water.
Working quickly, dip the truffles in the melted
dark chocolate using a fork. Return to the tray.
Sprinkle the tops with the remaining chopped
hazelnuts. Refrigerate for 1 hour, or until firm.

*Making your own chocolates isn't difficult,
and the results will be appreciated for a
special occasion or as a gift.*

CHOCOLATE DRINKS

*H*ere are some tempting drinks for chocolate lovers of all ages. Whatever the season, you'll find one to warm you up or cool you down.

CHOCOLATE MILK SHAKE

2 cups (500 ml) milk
2 scoops vanilla ice-cream
2 tablespoons chocolate syrup

··• PREPARATION 5 minutes
··• COOKING Nil
··• SERVES 2

In a blender, combine milk, ice-cream and chocolate syrup and blend until mixture is smooth and frothy. Pour into 2 tall glasses and serve.

CHOCOLATE THICK SHAKE

2 scoops chocolate ice-cream, homemade
    (see page 235) or shop-bought
100 g (3½ oz) dark chocolate, chopped
½ cup (125 ml) whipped cream
1 tablespoon chocolate shavings,
    to garnish

··• PREPARATION 5 minutes
··• COOKING Nil
··• SERVES 2

Blend the ice-cream, chocolate and half the whipped cream in a blender until smooth. Pour into 2 tall glasses, top with the remaining whipped cream and sprinkle with chocolate shavings.

Cinnamon cocoa

3 cups (750 ml) milk
1 cinnamon stick
¼ cup (30 g) unsweetened cocoa powder
85 g (3 oz) dark chocolate, chopped
ground cinnamon (optional), to serve

⁘ PREPARATION 5 minutes
⁘ COOKING Nil
⁘ SERVES 2

1 Heat the milk and cinnamon stick in a small saucepan over low heat. Bring to a simmer; do not boil or a skin will form. Remove from heat.

2 Sift the cocoa into a small heatproof bowl or jug (pitcher). Pour in the warm cinnamon milk. Remove the cinnamon stick, then add the chocolate, whisking for 3–4 minutes, or until well combined. Pour into heatproof serving glasses or mugs. Sprinkle with a little ground cinnamon if desired, and serve.

Mexican-style hot chocolate

1 cup (250 ml) pouring cream
2 cups (500 ml) full-cream (whole) milk
1 cup (250 ml) low-fat milk
½ cup (115 g) firmly packed dark brown sugar
¼ cup (30 g) unsweetened cocoa powder
½ teaspoon ground ancho chilli pepper
¼ teaspoon ground cinnamon
85 g (3 oz) dark chocolate
1 teaspoon vanilla extract
⅓ cup (80 ml) thickened (heavy/double) whipping cream
¼ cup (30 g) icing (confectioners') sugar

⁘ PREPARATION 10 minutes
⁘ COOKING Nil
⁘ SERVES 4

1 In a saucepan over medium heat, whisk together the cream, milks, brown sugar, cocoa, chilli and cinnamon. Bring to a simmer and cook, stirring, for 1 minute.

2 Remove from the heat and stir in the chocolate and vanilla until the chocolate has melted. Keep warm over low heat.

3 Beat together the thickened cream and icing sugar until stiff peaks form.

4 Pour the hot chocolate into 4 mugs and top each with a generous dollop of whipped cream.

HOT CHOCOLATE

2 cups (500 ml) milk
85 g (3 oz) dark chocolate,
    chopped
sugar, to taste (optional)
white and pink marshmallows,
    to serve (optional)
grated chocolate, to serve

PREPARATION 3 minutes
COOKING 3 minutes
SERVES 2

1 Heat the milk in a small saucepan over low heat. Bring to a simmer; do not boil or a skin will form.

2 Add the chocolate and stir until melted and smooth. Use a whisk to make it frothy, if you like. Stir in a little sugar if desired.

3 Pour into tall heatproof serving glasses or mugs. Top with marshmallows, if desired, and sprinkle with grated chocolate.

If you like, omit the marshmallows and top with a spoonful of whipped cream.

Rich, dark, French-style hot chocolate makes an indulgent winter treat, especially when served with marshmallows.

HEAVENLY HOT CHOCOLATE

½ cup (125 ml) low-fat milk
½ cup (125 ml) low-fat evaporated milk
1½ teaspoons sugar
3 teaspoons unsweetened cocoa powder
white and pink mini marshmallows,
    to serve
grated chocolate, to serve

PREPARATION 2 minutes
COOKING 5 minutes
SERVES 1

1 In a small heavy saucepan, combine the milks and sugar; heat, uncovered, over low heat for about 5 minutes, or until the milk bubbles gently.

2 Meanwhile, in a 1 cup (250 ml) teacup or mug, mix the cocoa with 1 teaspoon water to form a thick paste.

3 When the milk is ready, slowly pour it into the cocoa paste, stirring until smooth. Top with marshmallows and sprinkle with grated chocolate. Serve immediately.

DESSERTS

DARK CHOCOLATE POTS WITH WHITE CHOCOLATE CREAM

*T*his silky, rich dessert of dark and white chocolate wouldn't look out of place in a restaurant, yet it's unbelievably easy and quick to make at home.

200 g (7 oz) dark chocolate
    (70 per cent cocoa), chopped
1¾ cups (425 ml) low-fat ready-
    made custard or vanilla crème
    anglaise (at room temperature)
1 tablespoon brandy
½ cup (125 ml) cream
30 g (1 oz) white chocolate,
    finely grated

⤙ **PREPARATION** 15 minutes plus
    chilling
⤙ **COOKING** Nil
⤙ **SERVES** 6

Dark chocolate with 70 per cent cocoa will give this dessert the best flavour.

1 Put six ramekins, small glass dishes or shallow tumblers in the freezer to chill.

2 Melt the dark chocolate in a heatproof bowl set over a saucepan of gently simmering water. Stir until melted and smooth — this will take about 3 minutes.

3 Pour in about one-third of the custard or crème anglaise and stir lightly. The chocolate will begin to thicken and become glossy, so do not overmix — a couple of large scooping stirs are enough. Pour in all the remaining custard and stir to combine it with the chocolate. Stir in the brandy. The mixture will thicken as the chocolate cools.

4 Spoon mixture into the chilled ramekins. Put in the freezer to chill for 20 minutes, or until set.

5 Whip the cream until it just begins to thicken and hold its shape. Stir in the grated white chocolate and chill the cream until needed. Spoon the cream onto the chocolate pots and serve immediately.

SOFT CHOCOLATE ORANGE CREAMS

Melt 150 g (5 oz) dark chocolate instead of 200 g (7 oz). Omit the brandy and add the grated zest of 1 orange and 2 tablespoons orange juice. Chill the pots in the freezer for 20 minutes.

These desserts are lighter and more softly set than the main recipe.

🍃 To break up chocolate quickly, slap the whole bar in its unopened wrapping on a work surface. Do this five or six times, holding the bar by different sides, then open the wrapping over a large bowl. The chocolate will be broken into very small pieces.

🍃 Top the desserts with a dollop of mascarpone (with or without the grated white chocolate) or serve with fresh berries or sliced fresh nectarines, peaches, mango or pineapple on the side.

🍃 This versatile chocolate custard mixture can be used as a filling for sponge cake or Madeira (pound) cake, in pastry tartlets topped with strawberries and whipped cream, or as a warm chocolate dip for fruit, biscuits (cookies), savoiardi (lady fingers) or Italian biscotti.

SELF-SAUCING CHOCOLATE PUDDINGS

3 tablespoons melted butter,
   plus extra for brushing
1 cup (150 g) self-raising flour
2 tablespoons unsweetened cocoa
   powder
½ cup (115 g) caster (superfine)
   sugar
1 egg
½ cup (125 ml) milk
1 teaspoon vanilla extract
½ cup (50 g) walnuts, roughly
   chopped
sifted icing (confectioners') sugar,
   for dusting
thick (heavy/double) cream,
   to serve

CHOCOLATE SAUCE

¾ cup (170 g) caster (superfine)
   sugar
¼ cup (30 g) unsweetened cocoa
   powder

- **PREPARATION** 15 minutes
- **COOKING** 25 minutes
- **SERVES** 6

1 Preheat the oven to 180°C (350°F/Gas 4).
Brush the base and sides of six 1⅓ cup (330 ml)
capacity ramekins or heatproof dishes with
melted butter.

2 Sift the flour and cocoa into a bowl. Stir in the
sugar. Whisk together the extra 3 tablespoons
melted butter, the egg, milk and vanilla, then
pour into the flour mixture and stir until smooth.
Add the walnuts and mix lightly. Carefully spoon
or pour the mixture into the ramekins.

3 To make the chocolate sauce, put the sugar
and cocoa in a bowl, add 2 cups (500 ml) boiling
water and stir well to dissolve the sugar.

4 Slowly pour the chocolate sauce over each
pudding, then bake for 25 minutes. Dust the
puddings with icing sugar and serve with a
dollop of thick cream.

You can also make one large pudding,
using an 8 cup (2 litre) baking dish. Increase the
cooking time to 40 minutes.

These indulgent little puddings are deliciously rich, with a wonderful chocolate flavour. They are also very economical to make.

ORANGE CHOCOLATE MOUSSE

*asy to make, this dessert looks very elegant.
Its velvety texture and a hint of orange
flavour make a perfect ending to any meal.*

2 eggs, beaten

2 egg yolks, beaten

1 cup (250 ml) thickened (heavy/
    double) whipping cream

¼ cup (55 g) firmly packed brown
    sugar

3 tablespoons orange juice

1½ teaspoons grated orange zest

175 g (6 oz) dark chocolate,
    melted and cooled

orange zest, to garnish

whipped cream, to serve

·•· PREPARATION 20 minutes

·•· COOKING Nil

·•· SERVES 4

1 In a saucepan, combine the eggs, egg yolks, cream, sugar, orange juice and zest until blended. Cook, stirring, over low–medium heat for 15 minutes, or until the mixture has thickened.

2 Remove from the heat and stir in the melted chocolate until smooth. Pour into dessert dishes. Refrigerate for at least 2 hours before serving.

3 Garnish with orange zest and serve with whipped cream.

SAUCY CHOCOLATE PUDDINGS

75 g (2½ oz) self-raising flour
⅓ cup (40 g) unsweetened cocoa
    powder, plus extra for dusting
½ cup (95 g) lightly packed soft
    brown sugar
¼ cup (60 ml) milk
1 egg
1½ cups (375 ml) boiling water,
    approximately
cream or vanilla ice-cream,
    to serve (optional)

⁖ PREPARATION 10 minutes
⁖ COOKING 15 minutes
⁖ SERVES 4

Serve the puddings hot, before the sauce that forms at the bottom of each ramekin is absorbed back into the pudding.

1 Preheat the oven to 190°C (375°F/Gas 5). Lightly grease four 1¼ cup (300 ml) ovenproof ramekins. Sift the flour, half the cocoa and half the sugar into a bowl; make a well in the centre.

2 Whisk the milk and egg in a small bowl, then gently fold into the dry ingredients, using a rubber spatula. Spoon the batter into the ramekins.

3 Sift the remaining cocoa and sugar together, then sprinkle evenly over the batter in each ramekin. Set the ramekins on a baking tray and slowly pour ⅓ cup (80 ml) boiling water into each ramekin.

4 Bake for 15 minutes, or until the puddings feel firm on top. Dust with extra cocoa and serve immediately.

CHOC–HAZELNUT AND LIME STEAMED PUDDINGS

melted unsalted butter, for
    brushing
caster (superfine) sugar, for
    coating
6 thin slices lime, halved
3 tablespoons lime marmalade,
    warmed
100 g (3½ oz) dark chocolate
4 large eggs, separated
½ cup (115 g) caster (superfine)
    sugar
1 teaspoon vanilla essence
90 g (¾ cup) hazelnut meal
    (ground hazelnuts)
1 cup (60 g) fresh breadcrumbs
orange wedges, to garnish

CHOC–ORANGE SAUCE

100 g (3½ oz) dark chocolate
2 tablespoons icing
    (confectioners') sugar, sifted
½ cup (125 ml) thickened (heavy/
    double) whipping cream
1 tablespoon orange liqueur

⁎ **PREPARATION** 30 minutes
⁎ **COOKING** 4 minutes per batch
⁎ **SERVES** 6

1 Brush a 6-hole microwave-safe muffin tray with melted butter; coat with sugar, tipping out the excess. Place a half slice of lime and 1 teaspoon lime marmalade in the base of each muffin hole.

2 Melt the chocolate in the microwave oven on Defrost for 2 minutes. Stir, then melt on Defrost for a further 2 minutes. Continue this process until all the chocolate is melted.

3 Beat the egg yolks and caster sugar together until thick and creamy. Stir in the melted chocolate and vanilla.

4 Whisk the eggwhites with an electric mixer until soft peaks form. Fold the hazelnut meal, breadcrumbs and eggwhites into the chocolate mixture.

5 Spoon half the mixture evenly into the muffin holes. Place on a rack on the microwave turntable; cook on medium power for 4 minutes. Cover with paper towels and stand for 1 minute.

6 To make the sauce, melt the chocolate. Add the icing sugar, cream and liqueur and stir well. Turn out the puddings onto individual plates. Serve warm with the sauce.

Nuts are a natural accompaniment to chocolate, and the addition of citrus helps to cut the richness in these lovely puddings.

CLASSIC CHOCOLATE MOUSSE

250 g (8 oz) dark chocolate,
    broken into pieces
3 eggs, at room temperature,
    separated
300 ml (10 fl oz) cream, whipped,
    plus extra, to serve
chocolate scrolls (see page 13),
    to serve (optional)

•→ PREPARATION 20 minutes
        plus chilling
•→ COOKING Nil
•→ SERVES 6

 Add 2 tablespoons of your favourite liqueur or strong cold espresso, or 1 teaspoon vanilla extract, to the melted chocolate when adding the egg yolks.

 Serve these dark, smooth, decadent delights with some extra whipped cream, and fresh fruit such as sliced strawberries to cut the richness.

1 Melt the chocolate in a heatproof bowl set over a saucepan of barely simmering water, making sure the bottom of the bowl does not touch the water. Stand for about 3 minutes, stirring occasionally, to soften. Remove from the heat and stir until smooth.

2 Add the egg yolks to the chocolate and stir until smooth. Fold a little whipped cream through the chocolate mixture to loosen it, then fold in the remaining cream.

3 Using very clean electric beaters, beat the eggwhites until soft peaks form. Gently fold the eggwhites through the chocolate mixture using a large metal spoon or rubber spatula. Fold until all the white streaks are gone, but take care not to lose the volume.

4 Spoon the mixture into six ¾ cup (180 ml) glasses or small serving dishes. Cover with plastic wrap and refrigerate for 3 hours, or until thickened slightly and well chilled. Serve topped with whipped cream and shaved chocolate.

SURPRISE CHOCOLATE MOUSSE

*U*se a good-quality unsweetened cocoa powder (preferably Dutch cocoa) to ensure that the mousse has a rich chocolate taste.

¾ cup (120 g) pitted dates
1 large ripe avocado, peeled and roughly chopped
1 tablespoon maple syrup
⅓ cup (40 g) unsweetened cocoa powder
1 teaspoon vanilla extract

· **PREPARATION** 15 minutes plus standing and chilling
· **COOKING** Nil
· **SERVES** 4

1 Put the dates in a heatproof bowl. Cover with boiling water and stand for 10 minutes, or until softened. Drain, reserving the soaking liquid.

2 Process the dates in a food processor or blender until smooth. Add the avocado and process until smooth. Add the maple syrup, cocoa and vanilla and process until well combined, adding a little reserved soaking liquid (about 2 tablespoons) to achieve the desired consistency.

3 Spoon the mousse into four ½ cup (125 ml) dessert glasses. Refrigerate for 1 hour, or until chilled. Serve cold.

Avocado in a dessert may sound surprising, but it makes a dairy-free version of chocolate mousse that contains only good fats and very little added sugar. It tastes rich and chocolatey and it is packed with anti-oxidants.

The surprise is that this mousse contains no cream or other dairy products. Plus it's gluten free and suitable for vegans.

CHOCOLATE LATTE COTTO

2 tablespoons unsweetened cocoa
   powder
2 teaspoons (7 g) powdered clear
   gelatin
3 cups (750 ml) low-fat milk
½ cup (115 g) firmly packed light
   brown sugar
30 g (1 oz) dark chocolate
grated nutmeg
dark chocolate shavings (optional)

PREPARATION 20 minutes
COOKING Nil
SERVES 6

1 Combine the cocoa and 2 tablespoons water in a small bowl, stirring until the cocoa is moistened. In a separate bowl, sprinkle the gelatin over 1 cup (250 ml) milk and stand for 5 minutes, or until the gelatin has softened.

2 Meanwhile, combine the remaining milk, sugar, chocolate and a good grating of nutmeg in a medium saucepan. Bring to a simmer and cook until the chocolate has melted. Remove from the heat; stir in the cocoa mixture.

3 Stir in the gelatin, return to the heat and cook for 3 minutes, or until the gelatin has just dissolved. Divide the mixture among six ¾ cup (180 ml) ramekins or glass dishes. Cool to room temperature, then chill for at least 4 hours. Decorate with shaved chocolate, if you like.

CHOCOLATE CARAMEL CREAM

*T*hese rich, indulgent desserts are guaranteed to delight chocoholics. They're ideal for a stress-free dinner as they can be made ahead of time.

½ cup (115 g) caster (superfine) sugar

185 g (6 oz) can evaporated milk

200 g (7 oz) dark chocolate, broken into pieces

3 eggs, separated

- PREPARATION 30 minutes plus chilling
- COOKING Nil
- SERVES 4

If you prefer, you can melt chocolate in a microwave oven. To do this, break the chocolate into squares, put in a microwave-safe bowl and microwave for 2–4 minutes on low power. The time will vary depending on the wattage of the microwave, so keep an eye on it. Stir well.

1 Put the sugar in a large heavy-based saucepan with 2 tablespoons of cold water. Heat gently, stirring occasionally, until the sugar dissolves, then simmer for 10–12 minutes, or until caramelised and a rich golden colour.

2 With the pan over a low heat, gradually and carefully (as the mixture will froth up), pour the evaporated milk into the pan and stir until the caramel dissolves into the milk. (The caramel will harden when the milk is first poured in, but will dissolve again on heating.) Remove from the heat and let cool.

3 Meanwhile, melt the chocolate in a heatproof bowl set over a saucepan of simmering water, ensuring the base of the bowl does not touch the water. Let cool for 5 minutes, then beat in one egg yolk at a time, then the caramel mixture.

4 Whisk the eggwhites in a clean bowl until soft peaks form, then gently fold them into the chocolate mixture. Divide among 4 serving dishes. Refrigerate for at least 1 hour.

CHOCOLATE SOUFFLÉ

60 g (2 oz) dark chocolate
60 g (2 oz) butter
60 g (2 oz) plain (all-purpose) flour
⅓ cup (75 g) sugar, plus
    1 teaspoon extra
¼ teaspoon salt
1 cup (250 ml) milk
3 eggs, separated
1 teaspoon vanilla extract
¼ teaspoon almond extract

SAUCE

1 cup (250 ml) thickened (heavy/
    double) whipping cream
¼ cup (30 g) icing (confectioners')
    sugar
¼ teaspoon vanilla extract

·•· PREPARATION 15 minutes
·•· COOKING 1 hour
·•· SERVES 6

1 Preheat the oven to 160°C (320°F/ Gas 2–3). In a heavy saucepan, melt chocolate and butter over low heat; stir until smooth. In a small bowl, combine flour, sugar and salt. Add milk; stir this mixture into the melted chocolate. Cook, stirring, over medium heat until bubbling and thickened. Reduce heat; cook, stirring, a further 2 minutes. Remove from heat.

2 In a small bowl, beat the egg yolks. Stir a little chocolate mixture into the yolks, then return all the yolk mixture to the pan, stirring constantly. Add extracts.

3 Beat the eggwhites using clean electric beaters until soft peaks form. Gradually beat in 1 teaspoon sugar on high speed until stiff peaks form. With a spatula, stir one-quarter of the eggwhites into the chocolate batter until no white streaks remain, then fold in remaining eggwhites.

4 Spoon the batter into a greased 6 cup (1.5 litre) baking dish. Place dish in a larger baking tray. Fill the tray with hot water to a depth of 2.5 cm (1 inch). Bake for 1 hour, or until a knife inserted near the centre comes out clean.

5 For the sauce, beat the cream in a chilled small bowl until it begins to thicken. Add the icing sugar and vanilla; beat until soft peaks form. Serve the soufflé hot with a dollop of sauce.

CHESTNUT BRANDY MOUSSE

250 g (8 oz) can unsweetened
  chestnut purée
2 tablespoons brandy
2 tablespoons icing
  (confectioners') sugar
1 cup (250 ml) thickened (heavy/
  double) whipping cream
50 g (1¾ oz) dark chocolate,
  grated

⋆ **PREPARATION** 20 minutes plus
  chilling
⋆ **COOKING** Nil
⋆ **SERVES** 4

1 In a large bowl, combine the chestnut purée, brandy and sugar. Beat thoroughly using either an electric beater or a hand-held balloon whisk, until the mixture is smooth.

2 In a bowl, whip the cream until it holds soft peaks, then fold it into the chestnut mixture. Add half the chocolate to the mixture.

3 Spoon the cream into 4 glasses, sprinkle with the rest of the chocolate, and chill for 15 minutes before serving.

Look for chestnut purée in the baking or nut aisle of the supermarket. Or, make it at home: put 1 cup shelled and peeled chestnuts (fresh, canned or jarred) in a small saucepan and cover with milk. Simmer over low heat until very tender, about 1 hour. Add more milk if needed to keep the chestnuts covered. Purée in a food processor or blender and press through a sieve.

HOT CHOCOLATE SOUFFLÉS WITH RUM

*T*hese little chocolate soufflés are a breeze
to make, and they look very impressive,
especially if made and served in pretty dishes.

3 teaspoons unsalted butter,
    softened, for greasing
1/3 cup (80 g) caster (superfine)
    sugar
1 cup (250 ml) milk
100 g (3½ oz) dark chocolate,
    broken into small pieces
5 eggs
2 tablespoons cornflour
    (cornstarch)
2 tablespoons thickened (heavy/
    double) whipping cream
2 tablespoons rum (optional)
1 tablespoon icing (confectioners')
    sugar, for sifting

⁌ PREPARATION 20 minutes
⁌ COOKING 8–10 minutes
⁌ SERVES 6

1 Carefully butter the inside and rims of four 1 cup (250 ml) soufflé dishes. Coat evenly with 1 tablespoon caster sugar.

2 Heat the milk and chocolate in a small saucepan over medium heat. Just before the milk comes to a boil, remove from the heat, cover and stand for 2–3 minutes, until the chocolate has melted.

3 Meanwhile, separate the eggs, put the whites into a large, clean bowl and set aside. Put 3 egg yolks into a small bowl (the other two are not needed and can be kept for another purpose).

4 Add 2 tablespoons caster sugar to the cornflour in a large pan, and over low heat gradually whisk in the chocolate milk to form a smooth paste. Then increase the heat, beating continuously, until the sauce boils and becomes stiff.

5 Remove from the heat and beat in the cream, rum and egg yolks. Scrape the mixture from the side of the pan with a spatula and cover with the lid to prevent a skin from forming, then put aside. (The soufflé base can be made ahead to this stage, then the remaining steps done just before you want to bake and serve.)

6 When ready to bake the soufflés, preheat the oven to 230°C (450°F/Gas 8). Put a baking tray into the oven to heat.

7 Whisk the eggwhites with an electric mixer until they form soft peaks. Add the remaining caster sugar and whisk again until the whites are stiff and shiny.

8 Fold a large spoonful of the eggwhites into the chocolate sauce, then gently fold in all the remaining eggwhites. Spoon the mixture into the soufflé dishes and put on the baking tray in the oven.

9 Bake for 8–10 minutes, or until well risen and lightly set, with soft centres. Remove from the oven, sift over the icing sugar, and serve immediately.

You can start preparing these soufflés before you begin your meal and finish them off while the main course is being cleared away. To do this, prepare the soufflés ahead of time to the end of step 6. Preheat the oven before you begin your meal. Then, when the main course is over, proceed with steps 7–9.

For successful soufflés, the oven must be very hot. Putting the ramekins on a preheated baking tray helps them to rise as high as possible. Do not open the oven until the end of the cooking time, or the soufflés may deflate.

CHOCOLATEY ORANGE AND BLUEBERRY SOUFFLÉS

250 g (8 oz) blueberries
(fresh or frozen)
2 eggs
4 tablespoons caster (superfine)
sugar
3 tablespoons plain (all-purpose)
flour
2 tablespoons unsweetened cocoa
powder
grated zest and juice of 1 orange
½ teaspoon icing (confectioners')
sugar, for dusting

- PREPARATION 10 minutes
- COOKING 12 minutes
- SERVES 4

1 Preheat the oven to 220°C (425°F/Gas 7).
Place four 1 cup (250 ml) ramekins on a baking
tray and divide the blueberries among them.

2 Separate the eggs, pouring the whites into
a thoroughly clean bowl and placing the yolks
in a separate bowl. Add the sugar, flour, cocoa,
orange zest and juice to the egg yolks and beat
to form a smooth batter. Beat the eggwhites
using an electric mixer until stiff peaks form.
Use a large metal spoon to fold the eggwhites
into the batter.

3 Spoon the batter over the blueberries, level
each surface and bake for 12 minutes, or until
the soufflés are risen and set. Dust with icing
sugar and serve immediately.

*A gooey soufflé is baked over a blueberry base,
proving that even such an irresistible dessert
can be good for you.*

๛ When whisking eggwhites, both the bowl and beaters must be totally clean, dry and grease free or the whites will not stiffen. Glass or ceramic bowls are best.

๛ If you are preparing this dessert ahead of time, mix the chocolate batter a couple of hours in advance, then cover and set aside until needed. Place the eggwhites in a separate bowl and whisk them just before folding into the batter.

๛ Try frozen raspberries or mixed berries in place of the blueberries.

CHOCOLATE BANANA SOUFFLÉS

*B*ananas are packed with potassium and are a key
ingredient for heart health. This soufflé makes
the most out of the delicious fruit.

4 large, very ripe bananas, peeled
and cut into 5 cm (2 inch)
chunks
¾ cup (165 g) raw (demerara)
sugar, plus 2 tablespoons extra
125 g (4 oz) dark chocolate, cut
into 5 mm (¼ inch) pieces
⅛ teaspoon ground cinnamon
6 large eggwhites
pinch salt

⋯ PREPARATION 25 minutes
⋯ COOKING 12–15 minutes
⋯ SERVES 8

1 Purée the bananas in a food processor
or blender. Measure 2 cups pureé and
set aside.

2 In a medium saucepan, bring ¼ cup
(60 ml) water and ½ cup (110 g) of the
sugar to a boil over low heat, stirring
occasionally. When the mixture boils,
stop stirring and continue cooking for
about 2 minutes, or until the syrup
thickens. Stir half the banana purée into
the syrup. Stir in the remaining purée
and increase the heat to medium. Remove
from the heat and stir in the chocolate
and cinnamon. Let stand for 1 minute
to melt the chocolate, then whisk until
smooth. Pour the mixture into a
heatproof bowl and cool to room
temperature, stirring occasionally.

4 Beat the eggwhites and salt using an electric mixer until the eggwhites just begin to hold a shape. Increase the speed to medium–high and beat in the remaining ¼ cup (55 g) sugar in a slow stream until the mixture holds a soft, glossy peak when the beaters are lifted.

5 Gently fold the banana mixture into the eggwhites, working quickly to prevent the eggwhites from deflating. Divide the batter evenly among the ramekins, filling each to within 5 mm (¼ inch) of the top. Bake for 12–15 minutes, or until well risen. Immediately remove the baking tray from the oven. Use oven mitts to transfer the ramekins to dessert plates and serve immediately.

3 Set a rack in the middle of the oven. Preheat the oven to 200°C (400°F/Gas 6). Grease eight 1 cup (250 ml) ramekins, then divide the extra 2 tablespoons sugar among the ramekins, turning them to coat the greased surfaces with sugar. Tip out any excess sugar. Set the ramekins on a baking tray.

For successful soufflés, keep in mind the basics: Grease the ramekins well, make individual soufflés instead of one large one, bake only until they are well risen and lightly browned, and serve the soufflés within seconds of taking them out of the oven (they begin to deflate immediately).

Don't worry if the banana purée goes brown while you're preparing the soufflés. The chocolate will hide any discolouration.

CHEAT'S TIRAMISU

250 g (8 oz) mascarpone, at room
    temperature
2 tablespoons icing
    (confectioners') sugar
1 cup (250 ml) strong black coffee
8 savoiardi (lady finger biscuits)
1½ teaspoons unsweetened cocoa
    powder

◦•• PREPARATION 10 minutes
◦•• COOKING Nil
◦•• SERVES 4

🍃 Add a layer of raspberries
after the first layer of mascarpone.

🍃 Make sure the coffee is
cooled to room temperature
before using. To do this quickly,
prepare the coffee with half the
boiling water, then use cold water
to make up the quantity to 1 cup
(250 ml). You can use a good-
quality instant coffee if you like.

1 Put the mascarpone in a bowl, sift the icing
sugar over it and mix gently.

2 Pour the coffee into a separate bowl. Dip a
biscuit into the coffee, turn to coat, then allow
the coffee to drain back into the bowl. Dip and
drain the biscuit again to ensure the coffee has
soaked through to the middle. Break the soaked
biscuit in half, then lay the halves in the base of
a ¾ cup (180 ml) serving glass or bowl. Repeat
with more biscuits and another three glasses.

3 Divide half the mascarpone mixture over the
biscuits. Repeat with the remaining biscuits to
make another layer in each glass. Top with a
final layer of mascarpone.

4 Sift the cocoa over the top. Serve immediately,
or cover with plastic wrap and chill for up to
4 hours.

MOCHA RICOTTA TIRAMISU

*T*his lower-fat version of the popular Italian
dessert uses a mixture of sweetened ricotta
and yogurt instead of mascarpone.

8 savoiardi (lady finger biscuits)
1 teaspoon espresso instant coffee
     granules
1/2 cup (125 ml) boiling water
2 tablespoons coffee liqueur
     or brandy
1 teaspoon caster (superfine)
     sugar
200 g (7 oz) reduced-fat ricotta
200 g (7 oz) Greek-style yogurt
3 tablespoons icing
     (confectioners') sugar, sifted
1 teaspoon vanilla essence
30 g (1 oz) dark chocolate (at least
     70 per cent cocoa), grated, to
     decorate

➡ PREPARATION 20 minutes plus
     chilling
➡ COOKING Nil
➡ SERVES 4

1 Break each of the savoiardi into 3 pieces, then divide evenly among four 1 cup (250 ml) glass tumblers or bowls.

2 In a small bowl, combine the coffee, boiling water, liqueur or brandy and caster sugar, and stir to dissolve. Pour evenly over the savoiardi. Leave to soak while you make the topping.

3 In a bowl using an electric mixer, beat the ricotta, yogurt, icing sugar and vanilla until smooth and creamy. Pile on top of the soaked savoiardi.

4 Sprinkle each dessert with grated chocolate. Cover and chill for at least 30 minutes (but no more than 3 hours) before serving.

🍃 Ricotta cheese is much lower in fat and kilojoules than creamy mascarpone, which is traditionally used in this dessert. Adding Greek-style yogurt to the ricotta provides creaminess without loading the fat content. For a very smooth texture, push the ricotta through a sieve before using.

🍃 Savoiardi are light, sweet sponge biscuits shaped like a finger. They are also known as sponge fingers or lady fingers.

Vary the flavour to your taste by experimenting with different types of liqueur, such as hazelnut, orange, cherry or raspberry.

POACHED FRUIT WITH WHITE CHOCOLATE SAUCE

85 g (3 oz) white chocolate
    bits (or a bar of white
    chocolate, broken into
    pieces)
1 cup (250 ml) apple juice
1 teaspoon caster (superfine)
    sugar
1 tablespoon brandy
8 small or 4 large figs
2 large peaches or nectarines
150 g (5 oz) crème fraîche
1 orange

• PREPARATION 20 minutes
• COOKING Nil
• SERVES 4

Crème fraîche gives smoothness to the sauce, which also contains orange zest for a tangy citrus flavour.

1 Melt the chocolate in a heatproof bowl set over a saucepan of simmering water, ensuring the bottom of the bowl does not touch the water. Stir occasionally until melted. Remove from the heat and set both the chocolate and the pan of water aside.

2 Meanwhile, combine the apple juice, sugar and brandy in a shallow saucepan or a frying pan with a lid. Bring to a boil, then reduce the heat.

3 Rinse the figs. If large, cut lengthwise into quarters; if small, cut in halves. Halve and stone the peaches or nectarines, then cut each half into four slices. Add the fruit to the apple juice, cover and poach gently for 4 minutes. If the skins come off the peaches or nectarines, remove them.

4 While the fruit is cooking, gradually stir the crème fraîche into the melted chocolate with a balloon whisk, then beat until smooth. Put the bowl back on the pan of hot water while you finish off the fruit.

5 Using a slotted spoon, transfer the fruit to a serving dish. Boil the juice for 5 minutes, or until reduced to a slightly heavy syrup, then pour it over the fruit.

6 While the syrup reduces, grate half the zest from the orange into the chocolate mixture, then add 2 tablespoons juice. Stir the sauce and serve with the fruit.

If you prefer, you can melt the white chocolate quickly in a microwave oven. Put the chocolate pieces into a bowl, heat on low power for 30 seconds, then stir. If lumps of unmelted chocolate remain, cook in further 10-second bursts, stirring after each burst, until smooth.

APPLE AND BANANA SALAD WITH CHOCOLATE SAUCE

60 g (2 oz) dark chocolate

½ cup (125 ml) thickened (heavy/ double) whipping cream

2 green apples, such as granny smith

2 tablespoons lemon juice

2 ripe bananas

icing (confectioners') sugar, for dusting

pinch ground cinnamon

8 pitted dried dates, sliced

2 teaspoons chocolate flakes or shavings

⁕ PREPARATION 15 minutes plus chilling

⁕ COOKING Nil

⁕ SERVES 4

1 Break the dark chocolate into pieces. Melt chocolate and cream in a heatproof bowl set over a saucepan of gently simmering water. Stir until the chocolate melts. Remove and let cool. Chill in the refrigerator for 2 hours.

2 Peel and quarter the apples, removing the seeds. Thinly slice the apple quarters and place in a bowl; add the lemon juice. Peel and slice the bananas and combine with the apples. Turn the fruit in the lemon juice to prevent browning.

3 Spoon fruit onto dessert plates or bowls and dust with icing sugar and cinnamon.

4 Beat the chocolate and cream mixture until semi-stiff. Spoon onto the fruit portions and top with dates and chocolate flakes.

Creamy chocolate sauce dolloped over bananas and apples makes a dessert that's both healthy and indulgent.

FRUIT WITH APRICOT–
CHOCOLATE CREAM

1 cup (250 g) unflavoured fromage
　　frais (see note)

2 tablespoons cream

2 tablespoons caster (superfine)
　　sugar

½ teaspoon vanilla extract

⅓ cup (45 g) dried apricot halves,
　　coarsely chopped

2 tablespoons chocolate chips or
　　finely chopped dark chocolate

2 pears, cut into thin wedges

2 apples, cut into thin wedges

•• PREPARATION 15 minutes
•• COOKING Nil
•• SERVES 4

1 Purée the fromage frais, cream, sugar and
vanilla in a food processor until smooth. Transfer
to a serving bowl and stir in the apricots and
chocolate chips.

2 Arrange the wedges of pear and apple on a
platter and place the dip bowl in the centre.
The dip can be kept, covered, in the refrigerator
for up to 1 day.

  Add blueberries or diced
strawberries to the dip. Use dried
mango instead of apricots.

  Fromage frais is a low-fat
alternative to cream. The best
substitute is quark, or use Greek-
style yogurt. Or blend equal parts
cottage cheese and natural (plain)
yogurt until smooth.

WARM CHERRY AND CHOCOLATE TRIFLE

6 biscotti or amaretti biscuits,
    about 175 g (6 oz)
425 g (15 oz) can pitted
    cherries in juice or syrup
150 g (5 oz) blueberries
2 tablespoons cornflour
    (cornstarch)
2 tablespoons unsweetened
    cocoa powder
300 ml (10 fl oz) low-fat milk
1 teaspoon vanilla extract
2 tablespoons sugar
⅓ cup (40 g) white chocolate
    chips

↞ PREPARATION 15 minutes

↞ COOKING Nil

↞ SERVES 4

Adding sugar to the sauce at the end of cooking stops it sticking to the pan. The sauce may seem too thick before the sugar is added, but as the sugar melts, the sauce will thin to the correct consistency.

1 Break the biscotti in half and put 3 halves in each of 4 dishes. Drain the cherries, reserving the juice. Spoon a little juice over the biscotti and leave to soak for 5 minutes before topping with the cherries and blueberries.

2 Whisk cornflour and cocoa with a little of the milk in a small saucepan. Gradually whisk in the remaining milk. Use a wooden spoon to scrape up any cornflour from the base of the pan.

3 Put the pan on a medium heat and bring the sauce to a boil, whisking continuously. Reduce the heat and simmer, stirring gently, for 2 minutes. Whisk in the vanilla and sugar.

4 Pour the sauce over the fruit. Sprinkle with the chocolate chips and serve.

FRUITY YOGURT WITH CHOCOLATE-CHIP NUT CRUNCH

⅓ cup (45 g) hazelnuts
4 chocolate-chip biscuits
2 tablespoons honey
2 small ripe bananas, sliced
4 dried apricots, chopped
500 g (1 lb) low-fat natural (plain) yogurt

▪▸ PREPARATION 10 minutes
▪▸ COOKING Nil
▪▸ SERVES 4

1 Toast the hazelnuts in a small saucepan over medium heat, stirring, for a few minutes, or until fragrant. Tip into a bowl and allow to cool, then chop. Put the biscuits in a plastic bag and crush coarsely using a rolling pin. Tip into the bowl with the hazelnuts. Add the honey and mix well.

2 Mix the bananas and apricots into the yogurt and divide among 4 bowls. Top with the biscuit, nut and honey mixture and serve.

✎ Try these other toppings with natural yogurt. To make praline, brush a baking tray or a piece of foil with oil. Heat 4 tablespoons sugar and ½ cup (45 g) flaked almonds in a frying pan until the sugar melts. Cook on high for 1½–2 minutes, watching carefully, as the sugar caramelises quickly once it melts. With a spatula, scrape all the nuts and caramel out onto the tray or foil as soon as they are brown. Leave to set, then break up and sprinkle over the yogurt (or ice-cream, rice pudding or semolina).

✎ To make a sherried apricot sauce, mix 4 tablespoons apricot jam with 4 tablespoons sweet sherry. Drizzle over the yogurt and sprinkle with toasted flaked almonds.

✎ To make a blackcurrant and ginger topping for Greek-style yogurt, peel and very finely chop 30 g (1 oz) fresh ginger. Combine with 80 ml (⅓ cup) blackcurrant syrup (such as Ribena) and swirl the mixture through the yogurt.

*Natural yogurt is great for quick desserts.
Add some fruit and a crunchy nut topping
and it will round off a meal nicely.*

CHOCOLATE FONDUE

1 cup (250 ml) low-fat evaporated
    milk
¼ cup (55 g) sugar
¼ cup (30 g) unsweetened cocoa
    powder
2 teaspoons vanilla extract
1 cup (170 g) dark chocolate chips
    (at least 60 per cent cocoa)
fresh fruit, such as whole
    strawberries, mandarin or
    orange segments, kiwi fruit
    slices and pineapple chunks

⤙ PREPARATION 15 minutes
⤙ COOKING Nil
⤙ SERVES 10

🍃 Fresh fruit is both healthy
and delicious, but it tastes even
better dipped in a warm sauce
made from dark chocolate.

1 In a small saucepan, whisk together the milk,
sugar, cocoa and vanilla until well blended.
Add the chocolate chips.

2 Cook over low heat, stirring occasionally, until
melted, about 10 minutes. To serve, either pour
into a bowl and serve immediately, or pour into
a fondue pot (available at kitchenware shops) to
keep warm. Serve with fruit for dipping.

WICKED CHOCOLATE AND PECAN DIP

125 g (4 oz) plain chocolate,
broken into pieces
4 teaspoons honey or maple syrup
½ cup (125 g) fromage frais (or
blend ¼ cup/60 g yogurt with
¼ cup/60 g cottage cheese)
½ cup (60 g) pecans, finely
chopped
fresh fruit to serve, such as
cherries, pineapple chunks,
mandarin or orange segments,
strawberries, banana (about
185 g/6 oz per person)

··•· PREPARATION 15 minutes
··•· COOKING Nil
··•· SERVES 4

1 Melt the chocolate and honey in a small heatproof bowl set over a saucepan of barely simmering water for 5 minutes, stirring occasionally, until the chocolate has melted.

2 Remove the bowl from the pan and cool slightly. Stir in 2 tablespoons of the fromage frais and the pecans. Gradually stir in the remaining fromage frais and transfer the dipping sauce to a large serving bowl or 4 individual bowls.

3 Prepare a selection of fresh fruit to serve with the warm dipping sauce. Cut the fruit into bite-sized pieces and arrange on a serving dish.

To prevent chocolate from splitting when it is being melted, use a small saucepan that fits neatly under the bowl. It is essential to avoid getting water or steam in the chocolate because this will make the fat separate from the chocolate solids, causing the chocolate to solidify and become unusable. Do not overheat chocolate.

For added warmth, add a pinch of ground cinnamon, ground mixed spice or grated nutmeg to the chocolate with the nuts.

GINGER CHOCOLATE TEMPTATION

2 cups (500 ml) thick (heavy/
  double) cream
1 vanilla bean, split lengthwise
250 g (8 oz) dark chocolate,
  chopped
6 egg yolks, beaten
¼ cup (50 g) finely chopped glacé
  (candied) or crystallised ginger
whipped cream, to serve
  (optional)

- **PREPARATION** 15 minutes plus
  chilling
- **COOKING** Nil
- **SERVES** 12

1 In a small heavy saucepan, combine the cream and vanilla bean. Bring to a boil, then reduce the heat and simmer, uncovered, for 5 minutes.

2 Remove the vanilla bean and scrape the inside of the bean to remove the seeds; add the seeds to the pan. Discard the vanilla bean. Stir in the chocolate until melted.

3 Stir ½ cup of the chocolate mixture into the egg yolks; return all the mixture to the pan. Cook, stirring, until the mixture reaches 71°C (160°F) and thickens enough to coat the back of a metal spoon. Remove from the heat. Stir in 2 tablespoons ginger.

4 Pour into 12 demitasse or espresso cups. Refrigerate for at least 1 hour. Just before serving, garnish with whipped cream, if desired, and the remaining ginger.

This mousse-like dessert will be irresistible to all ginger lovers.

GINGER AND CHOCOLATE MASCARPONE

3 pieces ginger in syrup
2 tablespoons ginger syrup from the jar
2 tablespoons dark rum
100 g (3½ oz) dark chocolate
250 g (8 oz) mascarpone
4 brandy-snap baskets, to serve

• PREPARATION 10 minutes plus chilling
• COOKING Nil
• SERVES 4

1 Finely slice 1 piece ginger and put aside. Dice the remaining ginger finely and put into a bowl with the ginger syrup and the rum. Grate in the chocolate and stir to combine.

2 Add the mascarpone, mix well, then cover and chill for as long as you can. The mixture will stiffen as it chills.

3 Scoop the mixture into the brandy-snap baskets, top with the reserved ginger and serve.

Try brandy, sweet sherry or coffee liqueur as a substitute for the rum.

Brandy snap baskets are sweet baked casings made from sugar, golden syrup, butter, flour and ginger. Pre-made brandy-snap baskets are available from supermarkets.

A wickedly rich confection of dark chocolate, rum and creamy Italian cheese, studded with the sweet heat of ginger.

PEARS WITH CHOCOLATE SAUCE

*P*ears and chocolate are one of those classic, heavenly combinations. Enjoy this seductive dessert during the autumn months, when juicy pears are abundant.

1 cup (220 g) sugar
4 firm ripe pears
juice of 1 lemon
1 vanilla bean
100 ml (3½ fl oz) cream
100 g (3½ oz) dark chocolate, broken into pieces
1½ tablespoons orange liqueur or brandy (optional)

·•· PREPARATION 10 minutes
·•· COOKING About 25 minutes
·•· SERVES 4

Replace the liqueur in the sauce with fresh orange juice.

If the pears don't stand upright in the bowls, cut a thin slice from across the base to help steady them.

1 Put the sugar in a large saucepan with 4 cups (1 litre) of water. Dissolve over low heat, stirring constantly.

2 Leaving the stalk intact, peel the pears and remove the cores by cutting in through the base using a small knife or an apple corer. Sprinkle pears with lemon juice to prevent browning.

3 Split the vanilla bean in half, scrape the seeds into the sugar syrup, then add the bean. Bring the syrup to a boil, then add the pears. Reduce the heat and poach the pears for 15–20 minutes, or until they are just tender when tested with a skewer. Leave to cool in the syrup.

4 Shortly before serving, put the cream in a heatproof bowl. Add the chocolate and liqueur, if using, and heat over a saucepan of simmering water, stirring from time to time, until the chocolate has melted. Divide the hot sauce among serving bowls and sit a pear in each one. Serve immediately. (Reserve the pear poaching liquid to use in a fruit salad.)

CHOCOLATE BANANA SPLITS

*T*his healthier version of the good old banana split replaces whipped cream and toffeed walnuts with vanilla yogurt and pumpkin-seed crunch.

1 tablespoon white sugar
2 tablespoons pepitas (pumpkin seeds)
4 bananas
4 scoops vanilla frozen yogurt
¼ cup (60 ml) chocolate topping

•→ PREPARATION 10 minutes
•→ COOKING Nil
•→ SERVES 4

Pepitas (pumpkin seeds) are available from the health-food aisle of the supermarket.

Try a chocolate–strawberry split. Replace the bananas with 500 g (1 lb) strawberries, hulled and halved, and use strawberry frozen yogurt instead of vanilla.

1 Put the sugar in a small frying pan or saucepan over medium heat. Cook without stirring, shaking the pan occasionally, until the sugar has melted and is amber in colour, about 5 minutes.

2 Meanwhile, spray a baking tray and a large spoon with cooking oil.

3 As soon as the sugar is amber, immediately add the pepitas, remove from the heat, then stir for about 1 minute, or until the seeds are coated. Transfer to a baking try, spreading the pepitas out with the oiled spoon. When cool enough to handle, break up the pepita brittle.

4 Peel and thickly slice the bananas crosswise on the diagonal and divide among 4 dessert bowls. Add a scoop of frozen yogurt to each bowl. Drizzle with chocolate topping, then sprinkle the pepita brittle over the top.

This childhood favourite dessert gets a healthy
makeover without losing its appeal.

DARK CHOCOLATE ICE-CREAM

1 vanilla bean

1 cup (250 ml) milk

2/3 cup (145 g) caster (superfine) sugar

4 large egg yolks

2 tablespoons Dutch cocoa powder, sifted

100 g (3½ oz) dark chocolate, chopped

300 ml (10 fl oz) thickened (heavy/double) whipping cream

4 teaspoons chopped pistachios

PREPARATION 20 minutes plus chilling and churning

COOKING Nil

MAKES About 4 cups (1 litre)

1 Halve the vanilla bean and scrape the seeds into a saucepan. Add the milk and heat until hot.

2 Beat the sugar, egg yolks and cocoa in a heatproof bowl.

3 Pour half the hot milk over the egg mixture, whisking constantly, and return to the saucepan. Stir with a wooden spoon over low heat until the custard reaches 80°C (176°F), or thickens enough to coat the back of the spoon.

4 Meanwhile, melt the chocolate in a heatproof bowl set over a saucepan of hot water.

5 Remove the custard from the heat and strain into a clean bowl. Stir in the melted chocolate and the cream. Cool, then cover with plastic wrap and refrigerate for 4 hours or overnight.

6 Churn in an ice-cream machine according to the manufacturer's instructions. Sprinkle with chopped pistachios before serving.

Flavoured with vanilla seeds and dark chocolate, this ice-cream is rich and lush, ideal for a special occasion.

ROCKY ROAD ICE-CREAM

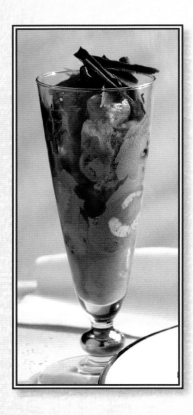

¹/₄ cup (40 g) chopped almonds, lightly
    toasted
¹/₄ cup (30 g) seedless raisins
60 g (2 oz) miniature marshmallows
4 scoops chocolate or chocolate chip
    ice-cream, slightly softened
whipped cream, to serve
chocolate sauce, to serve
chocolate curls (see page 13)

•➤• PREPARATION 10 minutes
•➤• COOKING Nil
•➤• SERVES 4

Stir the almonds, raisins and marshmallows into
the softened ice-cream. Spoon into tall glasses.
Return to the freezer for 10 minutes to firm
before serving with whipped cream, chocolate
sauce and a few chocolate curls to decorate.

CHOCOLATE ALMOND ICE-CREAM WEDGES

*H*ere's a fuss-free treat that looks impressive
but is fun to make, and takes only
15 minutes of your time.

1 cup (110 g) crushed amaretti cookies
4 scoops chocolate ice-cream
4 tablespoons ready-made chocolate fudge topping
4 tablespoons whipped cream
4 glacé (candied) cherries

•→ **PREPARATION** 15 minutes
•→ **COOKING** Nil
•→ **SERVES** 4

1 Place the cookie crumbs on a sheet of baking (parchment) paper. Roll the scoops of ice-cream in the crumbs. Place the ice-cream balls on a plate and refreeze until firm.

2 Spread a thin layer of the chocolate topping on four small plates. Cut each ice-cream ball into 4 wedges. Arrange the wedges on each plate. Add a dollop of whipped cream and a cherry.

Amaretti are small Italian almond cookies available in many supermarkets. If you can't find them, use crushed almond biscotti or Chinese almond cookies. Or change the flavour by using crushed digestive biscuits (graham crackers).

PEPPERMINT CHOCOLATE-CHIP ICE-CREAM

Bought ice-cream can never compare with the rich flavour and creamy texture of the homemade version.

1 cup (220 g) sugar

1¼ cups (310 ml) milk

3 egg yolks

2½ cups (625 ml) thick (heavy/ double) cream

1–2 teaspoons peppermint essence

200 g (7 oz) dark chocolate, finely chopped

few drops green food colouring (optional)

chocolate syrup, to serve (optional)

PREPARATION 30 minutes plus cooling and churning

COOKING Nil

MAKES About 4 cups (1 litre)

1 In a saucepan, lightly whisk together the sugar, milk and egg yolks. Stir over low heat until the sugar has dissolved. Stirring continuously, bring the mixture almost to a boil, then remove from the heat and allow to cool completely.

2 Stir the cream into the cooled custard mixture and add the peppermint essence to taste. Stir in the chocolate and add a few drops of the green food colouring, if using.

3 Churn in an ice-cream machine according to the manufacturer's instructions.

If you don't have an ice-cream maker, omit step 3. Instead, freeze the mixture in a metal tray until it has frozen 2–3 cm (about 1 inch) around the edges. Remove from the freezer, whisk well and return to the freezer. Repeat this process a further 4–6 times, then allow the ice-cream to freeze completely before serving.

For extra richness and an attractive presentation, drizzle chocolate sauce over the ice-cream just before serving.

CHOCOLATE ICE-CREAM CAKE

*T*ry this recipe if you like to have desserts on hand for unexpected guests or impromptu special occasions. It's easy, but looks very impressive.

·•· **PREPARATION** 25 minutes plus freezing

·•· **COOKING** Nil

·•· **SERVES** 10

CRUST

1 cup (100 g) vanilla wafer
    crumbs
½ cup (80 g) finely chopped
    peanuts
60 g (2 oz) unsalted butter, melted
2 tablespoons icing
    (confectioners') sugar

FILLING

6 cups (1.5 litres) chocolate
    ice-cream, softened
85 g (3 oz) cream cheese, softened
⅓ cup (90 g) crunchy peanut
    butter
¾ cup (90 g) icing
    (confectioners') sugar
¼ cup (60 ml) milk
½ cup (125 ml) cream, for
    whipping

1 Line the bottom and sides of a 13 x 18 cm (5 x 7 inch) loaf tin (bar pan) with foil.

2 For the crust, in a medium bowl, combine the wafer crumbs, peanuts, butter and icing sugar. Press half of the mixture into the bottom of the tin. Freeze for 15 minutes.

3 For the filling, remove the tin from the freezer and spread half of the ice-cream over the crust. Freeze until firm, about 1 hour.

4 Meanwhile, beat the cream cheese and peanut butter in a medium bowl. Add the sugar and milk; mix well. Whip the cream, then fold in. Spread this mixture over the ice-cream and freeze until firm, about 1 hour.

5 Spread with the remaining ice-cream (the tin will be very full). Press the remaining crumb mixture on the top. Cover and freeze for several hours or overnight.

6 Remove from the freezer 10 minutes before serving. Use the foil to lift the loaf from the pan, then remove and discard the foil. Cut into slices using a serrated knife.

Drizzle the top crust alternately with chocolate sauce and caramel sauce to create a decorative pattern.

To store this dessert to keep on hand, remove it from the tin and wrap the foil around it rather than peeling it off. Wrap in another layer of foil so that it is completely airtight, then store in the freezer until needed.

ICE-CREAM SANDWICHES

200 g (7 oz) almond meal (ground almonds)
300 g (10 oz) pure icing (confectioners') sugar
40 g (1½ oz) Dutch cocoa powder
5 large eggwhites
pinch cream of tartar
⅓ cup (80 g) caster (superfine) sugar
6 cups (1.5 litres) vanilla ice-cream
cinnamon and cocoa powder, for dusting
raspberries and mint leaves, to garnish

⤙ **PREPARATION** 15 minutes
⤙ **COOKING** 25 minutes
⤙ **MAKES** About 20

Have good-quality vanilla ice-cream on hand for this impressive dessert for a crowd.

1 Preheat the oven to 150°C (300°F/Gas 2). Line 2 baking trays with baking (parchment) paper.

2 In a large bowl using an electric mixer, beat the almond meal, icing sugar and cocoa on low speed until combined. Pass the mixture through a sieve onto baking paper.

3 Whisk eggwhites and cream of tartar until soft peaks form. While beating, gradually add the caster sugar and beat until the sugar is dissolved. Using a rubber spatula, gently fold the almond mixture into the eggwhites, one-third at a time.

4 Spoon the mixture onto the prepared trays in 3 cm (1¼ inch) rounds, allowing room for spreading. Alternatively, use a piping (icing) bag fitted with a 1 cm (½ inch) plain nozzle. Smooth out any peaks. Leave to rest for at least 30 minutes.

5 Bake for 25 minutes, or until puffed and crusted a little. Cool for 10–15 minutes on the trays, then transfer to a serving platter.

6 Fill each sandwich with 1 small scoop of vanilla ice-cream. Dust with cinnamon and cocoa. Garnish with mint leaves and raspberries and serve immediately.

LOW-FAT CHOCOLATE SAUCE

1½ tablespoons sugar
3 teaspoons cornflour (cornstarch)
½ cup (125 ml) low-fat milk
½ cup (160 ml) low-fat evaporated milk
30 g (1 oz) dark chocolate, grated
½ teaspoon vanilla extract

⁂ **MAKES** About 1 cup (250 ml)

1 In a small heavy saucepan, combine the sugar and cornflour and slowly add the milk and evaporated milk. Blend until smooth, then place over medium heat and cook, stirring constantly, for 3–5 minutes, or until thickened and smooth.

2 Transfer to a small bowl and stir in the chocolate and vanilla; stir until the chocolate is melted. Cover and cool.

୬୬ To make a mocha sauce, prepare as directed, but add 2 teaspoons instant coffee to the sugar–cornflour mixture.

୬୬ To make a chocolate and orange sauce, prepare as directed, but stir 1 teaspoon finely grated orange zest into the sauce together with the vanilla.

For Basic Chocolate Sauce (opposite), melt 100 g (3½ oz) chocolate in 150 ml (5 fl oz) hot milk or cream. Stir to melt the chocolate. Leave to cool.

*Whether hot or cold, a chocolate sauce
is a simple but effective way to dress up fruit,
ice-cream or a ready-made cake.*

BASIC CHOCOLATE SAUCE

150 ml (5 fl oz) milk or cream
100 g (3½ oz) dark chocolate,
    broken into pieces

•►• **MAKES** About 1 cup (250 ml)

1 Bring the milk or cream almost to a boil in a small saucepan over low heat.

2 Add the chocolate and stir gently until the chocolate is melted. Cover and cool before using.

CHOCOLATE–HONEY SAUCE

100 g (3½ oz) dark chocolate,
    broken into pieces
1 tablespoon unsalted butter
2 tablespoons honey or golden syrup

•►• **MAKES** About ½ cup (125 ml)

Put the chocolate in a small saucepan with the butter, honey or syrup and 1½ tablespoons water. Warm gently over low heat until the chocolate has melted. Serve warm.

CHOCOLATE FUDGE SAUCE

½ cup (125 ml) cream
1 tablespoon butter
¼ cup (45 g) lightly packed soft brown
    sugar
100 g (3½ oz) dark chocolate
1 teaspoon vanilla extract

•►• **MAKES** About 1 cup (250 ml)

1 Combine the cream, butter and sugar in a small saucepan. Stir over low–medium heat until the butter has melted and the sugar has dissolved. Bring to a boil, then remove from the heat.

2 Break up the chocolate, add to the pan and stand for 5 minutes, or until it has softened. Stir until smooth, then stir in the vanilla.

Serve this sauce warm over ice-cream, crepes or pancakes, or serve with any steamed pudding or berry dessert.

CHOC–CARAMEL SAUCE

1 large Mars bar, sliced
150 ml (5 fl oz) milk or pouring cream

•→• MAKES About 1 cup (250 ml)

Heat the Mars bar pieces and milk or
cream in a heatproof bowl set over a
saucepan of hot water. Stir until melted.
Pour immediately over vanilla ice-cream.

CHOCOLATE LIQUEUR SAUCE

1/2 cup (125 ml) cream
150 g (5 oz) dark chocolate, broken into
    pieces
1 tablespoon liqueur, such as Grand
    Marnier, Tia Maria or rum

•→• MAKES About 1½ cups (375 ml)

Bring the cream to a boil in a small
saucepan over medium heat. Remove
from the heat. Add the chocolate to the
pan and stand for 5 minutes, or until it
has softened. Stir until smooth, then stir
in the liqueur. Serve warm, or at room
temperature.

3-MINUTE FUDGE SAUCE

1/2 cup (60 g) unsweetened Dutch cocoa
    powder
3/4 cup (165 g) sugar
1/8 teaspoon salt
1/2 cup (125 ml) water (or use brewed
    coffee for more flavour)
1 tablespoon unsalted butter
1/4 teaspoon vanilla extract

•→• MAKES About 1 cup (250 ml)

Combine cocoa, sugar and salt in a small
saucepan. Add the water or coffee and
stir to mix. Bring to a boil over medium–
high heat, stirring constantly. Remove
from heat and stir in butter and vanilla
until the butter is melted. Serve warm.

⌁ Natural or 'non-alkalised' cocoa
powder has a natural acidity from the
cocoa beans from which it is made.
Dutch cocoa has an alkali added to
neutralise the acidity, mellowing the
flavour. Use natural cocoa for a stronger
chocolate flavour, especially in baked
goods or when the cocoa needs to stand
up to other strong-flavoured ingredients.
Choose Dutch cocoa when there are only
a few ingredients in the recipe or when
the acidity of natural cocoa may taste too
harsh, as when cocoa powder is dusted
over the surface of chocolate truffles.

Dark chocolate sauce

¾ cup (180 ml) thickened (heavy/double)
    whipping cream
200 g (7 oz) dark chocolate, roughly
    chopped
¼ cup (55 g) firmly packed soft brown
    sugar

⊷ **MAKES** 1½ cups (375 ml)

Place the cream, chocolate and sugar
in a heatproof bowl over a saucepan
of simmering water. Heat, stirring, for
3–4 minutes, or until the chocolate
almost melts. Remove the bowl from the
heat and continue to stir until all the
chocolate melts.

Quick chocolate sauce

1 cup (170 g) dark chocolate chips
¾ cup (180 ml) pouring cream
1 teaspoon vanilla extract

⊷ **MAKES** 1¼ cups (310 ml)

Put the chocolate chips and cream in a
small saucepan. Warm gently over low
heat, stirring constantly. Continue to
cook, stirring constantly, until the
chocolate is melted and the sauce is
smooth. Stir in the vanilla.

Vanilla chocolate syrup

300 g (10 oz) soft brown sugar
⅔ cup (150 ml) brewed coffee
60 g (2 oz) unsweetened cocoa powder
30 g (1 oz) milk chocolate, roughly
    chopped
pinch salt
30 ml (1 fl oz) vanilla extract

⊷ **MAKES** 1½ cups (375 ml)

1 In a medium saucepan, combine sugar,
coffee, cocoa, chocolate and salt. Whisk
constantly over medium heat until the
chocolate has melted and the cocoa has
completely dissolved.

2 Remove from heat and whisk in the
vanilla. Cool to room temperature. Store
in an airtight bottle or jar in the
refrigerator.

ICINGS AND GLAZES

A simple icing or glaze provides the finishing touch for your cake. These quantities make enough for an average-sized cake or 12 cupcakes.

WHITE CHOCOLATE GANACHE

180 g (6 oz) white chocolate, chopped
⅓ cup (80 ml) thickened (heavy/double) whipping cream

1 Place the chocolate and cream in a heatproof bowl over a saucepan of simmering water (make sure the bowl doesn't touch the water). Use a metal spoon to stir occasionally until chocolate melts and the mixture is smooth.

2 Place in the fridge for 1½ hours, stirring occasionally, or until the ganache is spreadable. Spread the ganache over the cake or cupcakes. Allow to set before serving.

VANILLA BUTTERCREAM

150 g (5 oz) unsalted butter, softened
1 teaspoon vanilla extract
1½ cups (185 g) icing (confectioners') sugar, sifted

Using an electric mixer, beat the butter and vanilla until light and creamy. Gradually beat in the icing sugar and continue beating until the mixture is light and fluffy. Spread the icing over the cake or cupcakes. Allow to set before serving.

For chocolate icings (frostings) and toppings, see pages 12, 17, 18, 22, 25, 26, 27, 30, 36, 46, 73, 100, 117, and 164.

For various chocolate ganache recipes, see pages 21, 30, 31 and 32.

White chocolate buttercream

125 g (4 oz) unsalted butter, softened
1 cup (125 g) icing (confectioners') sugar, sifted
125 g (4 oz) white chocolate, melted, cooled slightly

Using an electric mixer, beat the butter until light and creamy. Gradually beat in the icing sugar and continue beating until the mixture is light and fluffy. Add the melted chocolate and beat until combined. Spread the icing over the cake or cupcakes. Allow to set before serving.

Raspberry icing

125 g (4 oz) unsalted butter, softened
1⅓ cups (165 g) icing (confectioners') sugar, sifted
100 g (3½ oz) raspberries, puréed and strained

Using an electric mixer, beat the butter until light and creamy. Gradually beat in the icing sugar and continue beating until the mixture is light and fluffy. Add the raspberry purée and beat until combined. Spread the icing over the cake or cupcakes. Allow to set before serving.

Vanilla glaze

1½ cups (185 g) icing (confectioners') sugar
30 g (1 oz) unsalted butter, softened
1½ tablespoons hot water, or as needed

Sift the icing sugar into a medium bowl. Stir in the butter and enough hot water to make a smooth and spreadable paste. Spread the icing over the cake or cupcakes. Allow to set before serving.

Decoration ideas

❧ Sprinkle with silver cachous or top with bought coloured icing flowers.

❧ Chocolate drizzle: melt white or dark chocolate and place in a plastic snap-lock bag. Snip a hole in one corner of the bag to use like a piping (icing) bag.

❧ White or dark chocolate curls: melt chocolate and spread on a cold surface such as marble or a stainless-steel tray. Allow to set a little, then hold the blade of a sharp knife at a 70-degree angle on the chocolate and drag it towards you to create curls.

❧ Chocolate shavings: drag a vegetable peeler across the edge of a room-temperature block of chocolate.

INDEX

Note to readers

WEIGHTS AND MEASURES

Cup and spoon measures are level, unless stated otherwise. Ingredients are generally listed by their weight or volume with cup measurements given for convenience, unless the conversion is imperfect, in which case the ingredients are listed by weight or volume only.

Sometimes conversions within a recipe are not exact but are the closest conversion that is a suitable measurement for each system. Use either the metric or the imperial measurements; do not mix the two systems.

OVEN TEMPERATURES

These recipes have been written for a regular oven. If you have a fan-forced (convection) oven, reduce the temperature by 20°C (68°F). If you have a broiler (grill) where the temperature cannot be adjusted by a temperature dial or knob, lower the rack from the element as follows:
Medium: about half or two-thirds of the way down.
Medium–hot: about a third of the way down.

CAN SIZES

Can sizes vary between countries and manufacturers; if the stated size is unavailable, use the nearest equivalent.
    For example: 225 g = 8 oz; 300 g = 10 oz; 350 g = 12 oz; 400/410 g = 14 oz = 398 ml/410 ml; 425 g = 15 oz = 540 ml; 800 g = 28 oz = 796 ml.

ALTERNATIVE TERMS AND SUBSTITUTES

baking tray – baking sheet
benchtop – countertop
cream – where type of cream is not specified,
    use pure, light, single or pouring cream
cream cheese – soft cheese
filo – phyllo
gelatin – gelatine
icing – frosting
light evaporated milk – low-fat evaporated milk
low-fat milk – 1% milk
milk – where type of milk is not specified, use
    full-cream (whole) milk
pepitas (pumpkin seeds) – use sunflower seeds
self-raising flour – self-rising flour
sugar – use white (granulated) sugar unless
    otherwise stated
vanilla extract – vanilla essence
vegetable oil – use canola oil
wholemeal – whole-wheat

THE CHOCOLATE LOVER'S COOKBOOK

RECIPES Grace Campbell, Peta Dent,
  Michelle Earl, Cheryl Hingley,
  Cathie Lonnie, Maureen McKeon

COPY EDITOR Janine Flew

SENIOR DESIGNER Donna Heldon

DESIGNER Susanne Geppert

PROOFREADER Susan McCreery

INDEXER Diane Harriman

TRANSLATOR Avril Janks

PRODUCTION CONTROLLER Monique Tesoriero

PHOTOGRAPHER Steve Brown (pp 10, 12 top, 16, 19, 24, 71, 72, 77, 152, 163, 167, 178, 182, 185, 234, 242)

STYLIST Trish Heagerty

HOME ECONOMIST Peta Dent

**EDITORIAL PROJECT MANAGER
  GENERAL BOOKS** Deborah Nixon

READER'S DIGEST GENERAL BOOKS

EDITORIAL DIRECTOR Lynn Lewis

MANAGING EDITOR Rosemary McDonald

ART DIRECTOR Carole Orbell

Reader's Digest (Australia) Pty Limited,
80 Bay Street, Ultimo NSW 2007, Australia
www.readersdigest.com.au, www.readersdigest.co.nz,
www.readersdigest.co.za, www.rdasia.com,
www.readersdigest.co.uk, www.rd.com, www.readersdigest.ca

This edition first published 2013

The Chocolate Lover's Cookbook contains some material
first published in other Reader's Digest books.

National Library of Australia Cataloguing-in-Publication entry
  Title: The Chocolate Lover's Cookbook
  ISBN: 978-1-922083-12-8 (hbk.)
  ISBN: 978-1-922083-13-5 (pbk.)
  Notes: Includes index.
  Subjects: Cooking (Chocolate)
  Other Authors/Contributors: Reader's Digest (Australia)
  Dewey Number: 641.6374

Prepress by Sinnott Bros, Sydney
Printed and bound by Leo Paper Products, China

We are interested in receiving your comments on
the contents of this book. Write to:
The Editor, General Books Editorial,
Reader's Digest (Australia) Pty Limited,
GPO Box 4353, Sydney, NSW 2001,
or email us at bookeditors.au@readersdigest.com

To order additional copies of this book, please contact
us as follows:
www.readersdigest.com.au, 1300 300 030 (Australia);
www.readersdigest.co.nz, 0800 400 060 (New Zealand);
www.readersdigest.co.za, 0800 980 572 (South Africa);
www.rdasia.com; www.readersdigest.co.uk; www.rd.com;
www.readersdigest.ca;
or email us at customerservice@readersdigest.com.au

Concept code: AU 0916/IC
Product codes: 041 4831 (hbk), 041 4893 (pbk)